Conversations With Experts

Do What You Love, Get Paid What You're Worth

By

Caren Glasser and Friends

Dedication

Thank you to all my friends for contributing their time and knowledge. Without them, this book never would have come to fruition.

Conversations With Experts

TABLE OF CONTENTS

Introduction

PASSION: An intense desire or connection you have with someone or something. What is it that you really do or care strongly about?

PURPOSE: The vision you will use to shape that Passion and share it with others. What will you provide?

PROMOTION: The messaging and communication that connects and influences. How do you let your customers and prospects know and bring them in?

At Promote Your Passion™, it is our ongoing commitment to deliver valuable real-world ideas, knowledge, and skills that enable you to build a more profitable business through communicating from your customers' point of view.

Promote Your Passion™ events are fun, intense, content-rich, heart-centered, insightful, impactful, challenging, engaging, supportive and real-world practical – in short, jam-packed with strategies and tactics to help you Jump Start your business and take it to the next level.

This book is designed to accelerate your business growth by learning what is working today in Sales, Marketing, Social Media, On-Line Promotion, Networking and Motivation to grow your business. Read what the experts are saying about their passions.

Live with Passion!

Caren Glasser
Chief Passion Officer

Chapter 1
The Passion Force

By Caren Glasser

"When work, commitment, and pleasure all become one and you reach that deep well where passion lives, nothing is impossible."

You have a 9 to 5 job drawing a good pay, you have a good family and all's well with the world. But deep inside, you feel like you are going nowhere. The job isn't moving upward either. You are actually stagnating in your career, mentally and spiritually. Something is missing.

Passion. This is the one quality that textbooks, instruction manuals and company procedures will never talk about. Everyone is in such a hurry to make you fit perfectly into the machine like a well-oiled gear that they forgot you are a living, feeling human being. Even you have forgotten.

Ask yourself. If I had a million bucks in the bank, what kind of work would I be doing? Would I chuck this humdrum job and move on to something really exciting - something that I have always wanted to do? Then ask yourself – why am I not doing that right now? Is it because of peer pressure or because I don't want to move out of my comfort zone? Don't want to rock my boat? You are half asleep in your boat already, and in a few years you could be put out to pasture! If the boat rocks now, you could be jerked awake and come to your senses…. your passionate senses.

In the aftermath of the recession of 2008, millions of people lost their jobs. Many of them took up new vocations and suddenly found that they were finally following their dream. Many of them are now highly successful in their newfound professions.

You don't have to wait for dire straits to rock you out of your present mediocre life. You can decide right now that you want to live and work passionately and make your life worthwhile. The Highway of Passion is an amazing ride. And Prosperity is just one of the landmarks on this route! Get ready for the ride of your life!

Finding Your True Passion

> *"Nothing great in the world has been*
> *accomplished without passion.'*
> *– Georg Hegel, German philosopher*

So you have decided to break away from the monotony of your regular job. You want to live fully and passionately and reap all those rich rewards at the end of the rainbow. How do you find out what you are truly passionate about?

How do you separate the delusions from the do-able? You could be passionate about becoming the King of Spain, or winning the lottery or ruling the world. Indeed, there are people who have dreamt of that and done it. Alexander the Great ruled almost the entire known world in his time. But what is your true passion?

Here are a few steps you can take to discover the currents that move you deep inside:

1. Read your own body language. How does your body behave at your present job? Does it tense up and ache all the time? Do you get panic attacks very often? Are you so bored that you doze at your desk? Do you keep looking at the clock as break time approaches? Then you are in the wrong job. You simply don't have the passion for it. When you work on a job that you are passionate about, all your aches and cramps will dissolve. You will find yourself working extra hours, talking to your friends about your work and simply bubbling with life.

2. What did you love doing as a child? Your childhood hobbies and obsessions can indicate a genuine passion. Education and family pressures often move us away from our true calling. Did you love bikes or gardening or trekking? Then maybe a career in the automobile or landscaping or travel industries is where you should be! So sit back and recall your childhood and write down your memories. What made you smile then may still make you grin today, and in the future.

3. What do you love doing as an adult? You might very well have passionate side pursuits even today. Do you love your moonlighting job more than your regular day job? Many corporate honchos work the night shift as chefs or night school teachers. Start spending a few hours every day on your pet hobby. It may just hold the key to the real you!

Reviving Passion

"Rest in reason; move in passion"
– Khalil Gibran

Sometimes to unleash true passion in yourself, you may have to change your job to suit your aptitude better. But you may find that you do love your existing job, but simply don't feel very passionate about it. You can study your situation and then try to make a few changes to rekindle the passion you felt when you first started working.

Visualize yourself working passionately at your job. What would you be feeling? A sharp focus, clear vision of your future, total control and mastery over your work, a healthy body and an exuberant attitude! Then reverse engineer these symptoms to regain your passion.

Check on whether you work better with a team on the field rather than those solitary hours at a desk. Are you logical minded or creative minded? Are you crunching numbers when you would rather be in the design section? Get a revised aptitude assessment done. Ask your superior for a re-designation or transfer to a more appropriate department.

Exercise your body for at least thirty minutes every day. Let the adrenalin pump and flow in your blood. Eat healthy food and drink a lot of water. Quit smoking and using any stimulants. Restore the balance between your spirituality and physicality by meditation and prayer. Your refreshed body will invigorate your mind and passion will return.

Increase your knowledge of your field by taking new study courses. Take time out to travel and widen your perspective. Take a half-pay sabbatical to add new qualifications to your resume. Some lateral career movement can bring an innovative twist in your way of working.

Passion does not come overnight. Taking these proactive steps will see a gradual increase in your enthusiasm. You will begin working with a newly fired zeal, which becomes contagious, motivating your teammates as well. You will have consciously taken charge of your life again and the fruits of prosperity will be in sight once again.

The Passion Force

What drives passionate people to work so hard? Where do they get their energy? Passion can be fueled by many factors. Let us examine the 6 most important sources of the Force.

Passion Force 1 - Curiosity
One of the most powerful triggers of human invention has been curiosity. Why does something happen? How does lightning occur? What happens if you mix two chemicals? Which route will discover new lands? The human mind is programmed to question everything around it.

Passion Force 2 - Challenge
Our search for the sources of passion brings us to yet another powerful factor – Challenge.

A challenge can be posed by a person upon himself or by external forces. A personal challenge can arise from adverse circumstances of poverty or deprivation. Rags-to-riches stories have been told for hundreds of years now. Even Presidents of countries have risen from humble beginnings and risen to their positions of power by the sheer force of their passion.

Passion Force 3 - Legacy

When you are young, your motivation for working and living lies in larger income, better standards of living, and in general having a good time. But as you grow older, your priorities change. You want something more fulfilling. You seek to achieve goals that you will be remembered for. A sense of urgency begins to set in as time passes. And the source of your passion arises from wanting to leave behind a legacy.

Passion Force 4 – Faith

One of the most powerful engines of passion is faith in an external agency. Though faith may seem to have been marginalized in today's seemingly rational society, it still works behind the scenes in many areas.

Religion plays a dominant role in the lives of millions of people in the world today. Priests, nuns, monks, sadhus and mullahs are known to accomplish tremendous feats of social work and penance. Their faith in God and their religious ideals is the rocket fuel in their lives.

Passion Force 5 - Altruism

Altruism is defined as 'unselfish regard for or devotion to the welfare of others' and also 'behavior by an animal that is not beneficial to or may be harmful to itself, but that benefits others of its species'.

How does altruism become a force of passion? In the ongoing recession we have millions of jobs being lost. Many of these people have taken up volunteer work in social or environmental organizations. And quite a number of them have discovered that this selfless work gives them more satisfaction than their high paying job ever gave them. Their paradigm has shifted from the prosperity of the body to the prosperity of the soul.

Passion Force 6 – Epiphany

One of the definitions of epiphany is 'A comprehension or perception of reality by means of a sudden intuitive realization.' That's a moment in your life when you are suddenly struck by a powerful thought that changes your life forever.

A lifelong passion can be triggered by an epiphany. Such a life changing incident occurs in the lives of many great men. It may be something provocative that someone says to you. It may be the sight of another human being suffering. It can be a sudden realization that you hate your present job and you decide what you really want to do in life. Sometimes an epiphany can be a harsh tragic event like the demise of a family member, or some colossal disaster somewhere in the world. Your eyes open wide and all the shades fall off. You can see clearly around you and far ahead.

Your passion could be a great tool that could take you places.

Don't stifle it. Don't let it die.

Instead, give it the right fuel and watch it blaze like an inferno. This would be the inferno of your success.

About Caren Glasser

For the past 30 years Caren Glasser has dedicated her personal and professional life to communicating and connecting with people. Her past experiences have allowed her to meet many different people, and make a difference in their lives. In the early 90's she was a children's rock and roll singer, signed with Rhino Records. She traveled the country singing songs of self-esteem. That experience culminated with a concert at Carnegie hall. During that same time she owned a creative arts company that provided programming for the public and private schools sector in Los Angeles. She has learned a lot about what it takes to create positive experiences in our lives. Today, as the founder of Promote Your Passion™, she focuses on helping people find their passion and create better lives for themselves.

Caren Glasser, CPO Promote Your Passion

caren@promoteyourpassionnow.com
www.promoteyourpassionnow.com

Mobile 415.827.5358
Office 415.599.4475

Chapter Two
Giving the Customer More Than They Expect
By Casey Eberhart

O.K. So here I sit on an airplane traveling to Orlando, Florida to speak with some amazing entrepreneurs and to share what the promoters call "wisdom" and I have to say it has me really excited. What I thought I would do is share with you two core beliefs of mine and what I believe will be the new way of doing business in the future.

Let me start with a story to share with you the first of my core beliefs. My Grandfather was the true definition of an entrepreneur and I always looked up to him for as long as I can remember! His style was not multiple "streams" of income but multiple RAPIDS of income! So here is a little story to share my first main core business belief.

My Grandfather lived in a small one stoplight town called Fowler, Colorado. I used to visit there often as a kid. On one such trip, when I was just 5 years old, I asked him to teach me about business. Little did I know that that day my life would change forever! He put me on a tractor and we drove past the rental house he owned (rapid), past the Model A restoration garage next to it (rapid), past his Antique store (rapid), and then out into a pasture filled with land he owned (rapid), through his thousands of cattle (rapid), past his oil and gas wells (rapid), and finally out to the giant water well (rapid), where he turned off the tractor so we could "chat". It was there on that tractor that our chat resulted in my life changing! He got really quiet and said a phrase that changed my life. It has made me a lot of money, but more importantly it has made me who I am as a business professional today. He had made such a good build up, I really thought I was going to learn everything I needed to know about how to be a big business guru. And then it came, in one short sentence:

ALWAYS GIVE THE CUSTOMER WAY MORE VALUE THAN THEY EVER EXPECT TO RECEIVE AND EVERYTHING WILL BE O.K.

That was it?!? Seriously? I had ridden out into the middle of a smelly field to hear that? Yep, and in retrospect it was one of the best lessons I have ever learned! So now, the rest of what happened that day. He fired that rusty old tractor back up and drove back through the field to the Antique store where this principle would be put to the test. Now, I say "antique" store, but let's face it, if you have been to the Midwest, it should be called a "working garage sale!", but some marketer figured out calling them antique stores would sell more unwanted junk!! O.k., back to the store. A car pulled up the dusty driveway and two ladies got out of the car. I was now in charge of the store with his over site. The two ladies came up to the counter with these two insulators, which are glass things they used to put up on the top of telephone poles. They were a dollar each. I was so excited! I was about to make 2 dollars!! As a 5 year old, let's face it, that's some serious coin! I rang them up, took their money and glanced over to my grandfather for his approval. I remember him looking at me and raising one eyebrow as if I were to do something more. Then it hit me.

ALWAYS GIVE THE CUSTOMER WAY MORE VALUE THAN THEY EVER EXPECT TO RECEIVE AND EVERYTHING WILL BE O.K.
So here is what happened. I took these glass things (insulators) that would never break and wrapped them in newspaper,

wrapped that in bubble wrap and finally put the bubble wrap in a box. I put the box in a bag and thought I had given them tons of value because these things would never break anyways - it was total overkill! I looked over again for his approval and again saw the eyebrow!

ALWAYS GIVE THE CUSTOMER WAY MORE VALUE THAN THEY EVER EXPECT TO RECEIVE AND EVERYTHING WILL BE O.K.

O.K.! I got it. I offered to walk the bag out to the car and on the way I had a little idea. I asked the ladies to open the back door to the car and I proceeded to place the bag in the back seat and fastened the seatbelt around it! I then opened the door for both ladies, just to help them get in the car, and make their experience at the store stellar! Well, one of the ladies was so impressed, that she took out a nice crisp 20 dollar bill and handed it to me!! Are you kidding me? A 20 dollar bill to a 5 year old is like the whole bank!! I was HOOKED on business from that very second! I had given them so much value that they literally gave me 10 times the cost of the product because of the extra value I provided. Ever since that day, I have lived my life by the core belief I had learned that day in Fowler.

ALWAYS GIVE THE CUSTOMER WAY MORE VALUE THAN THEY EVER EXPECT TO RECEIVE AND EVERYTHING WILL BE O.K.

The story above is how I start every training session I do because I think so many people are not into providing extra value without charging for it, and that we as a society have forgotten how to really treat people like they did in the days of yesteryear!

~~~~~~

I would like to share with you another core philosophy of mine that has played a huge role in how I operate my business and my life. Here it is -- are you ready?

"CONNECTIVITY IS TODAY'S NEW CURRENCY"
Before reading another word, please re-read the above sentence. It is so important that if you get nothing else from this, please get that connectivity is really what runs the world! Think about it, you have heard many variations of this:

"It's not what you know but who you know."
"It's not who you know but who knows you."
"How big is your email list?"
"How many Facebook friends do you have?"
"How many twitter followers do you have?"
"How big is your Rolodex?" (Dating some of you!)
"Who do you know...."
"I got a guy...."
"I was referred by..."
"He's got connections."

You get the drift.

Here is the bottom line. The person who has the most and the deepest connections will most often win the game! I am a firm believer that they go hand in hand when it comes to business. It is not as easy to just say you can have lots of shallow connections (aka a HUGE email list) and still win in the game of business! There is a "Guru" that runs around telling people he is a "Guru" because he has an email list of over 400,000 people, and yet he gets next to ZERO response when he sends out an email! Why? He never met my grandfather!! He gives almost no value at all! There are also people out there who have so much to give, tons and tons of value, but who don't know anyone outside their very own family!! The key is to be building relationships and adding value to those relationships at every single opportunity!

Here are a just a few things you can do to get better connected and give value at the same time:

1. Send someone an article that would help them in their business.
2. When you see an opportunity to recommend someone, do it!
3. Make it a habit on your social media sites to promote others one at a time.
4. Send out thank you cards.
5. Take out your mobile device and text someone right now that you appreciate them!
6. Meet at least 3 new people per day and see how you can add value to their lives.
7. Call the client you lost last month and let them know you are still sad they left.
8. Do what you say you are going to do.
9. While at networking events, introduce the "players" to each other.
10. Go out of your way to give your next 10 clients "WAY" more than they expect.

I value your time and hope you walk away from this with a better view of who I am as a person. If there is anything I can do to support you in your business, please connect with me on

Facebook at facebook.com/CaseyFan, check out my blog at **TheIdealNetworker.com,** or go straight to my main site at **CaseyEberhart.com**

Now, go out and give someone you just met an AWESOME day!!

About Casey Eberhart

Casey Dean Eberhart has been an entrepreneur since his first business venture at the age of five. At the age of 22 he was made General Manager of a $22 million amusement park. Between toddler and adult Casey majored in both Business Management and Human Resource Management at Washington State University. After graduating, Casey made his way to Los Angeles where he found himself working as a Production Manager/Line Producer on feature films including the Oscar winning best picture Being John Malkovich. With his well-earned success in film Casey started his own production equipment rental company, Atomic Production Supplies.

Casey's business ventures are in no way, shape or form limited to entertainment. His love of business and his love of the "art of the deal" have taken him into uncharted waters time and time again. He has owned businesses ranging from a lingerie store in an adult nightclub, to a Gymboree for the betterment of children, to an online T-shirt company. His need to learn and grow constantly forces him down new paths and at the onset of the real estate boom Casey made his mark with purchases of homes and condos in both Los Angeles and Las Vegas. His willingness to try something new and his desire for knowledge is his catalyst for his continued success.

Business is a skill and Casey hones his skills with ongoing study of his trade. He is an avid member of Toastmasters Intl., a voracious reader of business development publications and he attends training conferences and seminars in a wide variety of fields. He is also part of Business Networking International, Long Beach Community Business Network, The Network for You, and many other organizations.

Casey is an established businessman and his drive for personal success has increased his drive for the success of his community and the world around him. With yet another venture, he has become a sender of cards, all kinds of cards. Send Out Cards is his way of bringing positive energy into the world around him. It allows him to explore an artistic, creative side, in exchange supporting his new passion for changing the world one card at a time. And, lest we not forget, in true Casey fashion, it is a fantastic business tool.

To connect with Casey about presenting to your group, team or organization, please use the info below:

Casey@TheIdealNetworker.com
www.CaseyEberhart.com
Facebook.com/CaseyFan
424-2-B-A-YAPPER **(424.222.9277)**
Give someone an AWESOME day!

Chapter 3
Always Be Marketing!
By David Asarnow

I'm sure you've heard about the old sales maxim, "Always be closing." Closing a sale is what businesses and business owners focus their time, effort, energy and money on. There is no doubt that "sales" is the lifeblood of business. Consistently increasing sales can grow a business to the next level. The truth is many entrepreneurs are laser-focused on closing sales that they neglect marketing their business. Unfortunately, marketing and advertising is usually the first thing that businesses cut back on when budgeting in lean economic times. Marketing and advertising can make or break a business.

The lack of marketing becomes evident when entrepreneurs are asked if they have a marketing calendar. For a business to last and thrive (even outlast the entrepreneur), it must have consistent and targeted marketing strategies. Although many businesses run a small ad in the newspaper once or twice a year, this should not be considered marketing. The best marketing is strategic and focused on attracting as many eyeballs as possible. An effective marketing lead generation process increases the chances for the sales team to close at a higher percent.

If you were to stand on a stage in front of hundreds of eager prospects, how would you introduce yourself? What would you tell them about you and your business that would convince them to buy from you or your business?

The challenge for most business owners is that when given the opportunity to introduce themselves they tell prospective clients what they sell or simply say what industry they are in. Your answer to that question should quickly educate any potential customer about how you, your concept, product, service or idea will impact and bring value to them. Your answer should also lead to questions that will allow them to see you as being the solution to their wants, needs and desires.

If using the "education based marketing" approach is not part of your typical current response, then you are not maximizing profit potential.

So let's break down the responsibilities of a business owner. The most important activities in your business should be as easy as 1-2-3:

1. Understanding your clients' wants, needs, and desires, and then providing the education-based information that supports you as their solution;
2. Creating compelling marketing for the concepts, products, services, and/or ideas;
3. Selling and delivering the promised result(s).

When the doors of your business are open, these should be the three areas of focus *every* day.

Most books on marketing talk about how to build a compelling brand, the old method, which worked when you could create a TV ad to monopolize the 4 – 7 stations in your media market. This is no longer an effective or cost-efficient model.

When you first opened your doors, you sat back and waited for customers to come rolling into your business with cash or credit card in hand. After all, your idea was a sure thing, right?

So when sales were slow to start, you probably turned to local newspapers, value clipper publications, magazines, and newsletters. Next, you looked at what the competition was doing, and you thought that if you offered your product or service at a lower price, customers would flock to your business instead of your competition. But what really happened?

Initially, you may have seen a rush of customers after you ran the promotion offering the product at a low price; however, did that rush of customers continue? Did they return after the sale was over? No.

As time went on, you probably did less and less advertising because you weren't seeing great results from your advertising dollars spent. You may have even bought into the false belief that you were just a small business owner, selling a gadget or providing a service, but not a marketer.

Entrepreneurs fail to realize that they have to become marketers. If you want to be a successful and profitable business owner, then your primary job every day is attracting more customers to your business.

Why? Because you need people to come to your business willing, ready, and able to pay you money in exchange for what you offer.

Other day-to-activities that do not bring in revenue can easily become the focus of a misguided small business owner. For example,

- You don't get paid when you counsel employees.
- You don't get paid when you do payroll.
- You don't get paid when you answer questions about when the next delivery truck will arrive.
- You don't get paid when you sit around all day hoping and praying that someone is going to walk into your business or pick up a phone and call you!

You get paid when a transaction occurs, when you deliver value in exchange for money. Because of this, your number one job as a business owner each and every day is to implement your business, sales and marketing strategy and to make sure the tactics you deploy are driving more paying customers through the doors. Once the customer enters, you should do everything possible to make sure you have an effective plan in place to capture their information and sell them again and again. Because of the outstanding job you and/or your team did, referrals start to come in. The only way to do this is to become a marketing and advertising enthusiast.

When you begin to embrace the role of marketer in your business, it will become very easy to see if you are using the right tactics in your marketing strategy. More importantly, this focus and attention will allow you to easily navigate any economic conditions that may arise. Having the marketing edge is what every business owner needs to run a business, regardless of how good the competition is.

Let's look at Wal-Mart and Nordstrom. These two companies compete against each other to attract customers. They are two department stores that reach out to each end of the economic spectrum. Wal-Mart specializes in discounted products, while Nordstrom focuses on customers who spend more for better quality.

Wal-Mart has created a reputable brand; with a broad range of products from apparel to groceries and toiletries, to automotive services. Wal-Mart also offers private labels such as Sam's Choice, Great Value, and Equate. They also offer suppliers exposure to a huge number of customers everyday at a discounted price.

Unlike Wal-Mart, Nordstrom does not offer toiletries or groceries. They do offer higher end apparel and home décor, and at full retail price. Nordstrom's goal is to offer a range of high quality upscale long lasting products for all types of customers.

Wal-Mart's branding is discount while Nordstrom focuses on high quality and high retail price. Although Wal-Mart and Nordstrom's are huge companies, their marketing is strategic. They consistently cater their message to their consumers.

Marketing is crucial in every business. But that does not mean that you will implement the same marketing strategies over and over again. The key to a great marketing strategy is to run different campaigns all the time, and to continually put new information in front of your clients.

The most successful businesses know that presenting fresh content to current and potential customers increases curiosity. Marketing is so crucial to your business that you should have different campaigns in play at all times.

The questions you may be asking at this point are, "Isn't that excessive? Won't that just overload my customers?"

The answer to each of those questions is exactly the same: "Not if your marketing is good."

If your marketing is effective, then your customers will never feel like they are being "sold." With the right marketing strategies, prospects and customers will not tire of seeing your ads because you are bringing them value.

Many businesses avoid marketing and advertising because they believe it is too expensive. A common misnomer about marketing is associating it with huge expense.

This is no longer the case! With hundreds of channels on cable TV and other new media strategies, it is easy to get noticed. Even on a small budget you can compel prospects to take action through a well-targeted advertising campaign.

There are many ways to advertise your business on a small marketing budget. You will be amazed that many of them cost less than what you spend on lunch for a week. Actually, many of them are free.

Yes, I said F-R-E-E. You can afford that, right?

You MUST view yourself as the marketer of your business, not just the owner. When you do this, you have an opportunity to succeed in any economy.

When you create and implement an effective marketing strategy, you can dominate in your business.

To receive FREE business and marketing advice, please visit my website **www.BusinessGrowthFactors.com**.

About David Asarnow

David Asarnow, an authority in the area of accelerated business growth, has generated hundreds of millions of dollars in sales over the last twenty years. His clients have added millions of dollars to their bottom line after implementing David's practical business advice.

As Speaker, Author, Certified Business Coach and Master Business and Sales Trainer, David has trained thousands of business professionals worldwide.

It is David's passion to inspire others to believe in their dreams and their goals and to have the confidence to take direct and committed actions to achieve them. David's passions are his family, spirituality, the outdoors, and helping business owners understand the psychology of success, and how to incorporate it strategically in growing their business.

Many of America's top companies regularly hire David to train, motivate and inspire their teams to build their business like a champion. You can learn more about David and his approach to business and life success at **www.DavidAsarnow.com**

Chapter 4
The Three Key Elements to Growing Your Sales Online
By David B. Wright

Growing your sales online is actually pretty simple. There are three main components to this: getting found, getting visitors to your website, and converting those visitors to customers. While this might seem overly simplistic, I'm trying to keep it simple enough to help you take action on it and increase your sales – then you can implement more complex tactics as you grow. If you're already an advanced marketer, there still may be some useful nuggets here.

Since I love to over-deliver, we'll also cover a bonus fourth element: selling more to those customers, more often.

The First Step Is To Get Found.

If no one knows how to buy from you, let alone who you are and what you've got for sale, it's going to be a challenge to make the sale, to say the least. Woody Allen once said, "90% of life is just showing up." But for our purposes, we'll use an oft-repeated version of this: "90% of success is just showing up." In online sales, showing up means getting found online. Getting found online means showing up when your prospective customers are looking for what you have to offer – and, ideally, when they're ready to buy, not just browse or research. There are a number of ways to show up online – and these range from simple to complex.

One simple way to get found is buying ads. There are many types of ads to choose from, but the concept and execution is pretty simple. Of course, there are elements of any ad that need to be tested to optimize conversion, but ads can be a quick and effective way to get people to your website. Try advertising where your target market already goes for information – such as email newsletters they read.

One of the more effective, yet more complex ways to drive visitor traffic to your website is called Search Engine Optimization, or SEO. Basically what this means is getting to the first page of Google and other search engines for key words & phrases your clients are searching for. An advantage of SEO is that the "organic" results on the search engines tend to be perceived as more credible and trustworthy than the ads that appear on the same pages.

There are many other ways to get found, including video (and video SEO), social media, pay-per-click (PPC) ads, banner ads, newsletters, press releases, media coverage, local search (think SEO for a local geographic area), tying offline ads to online marketing (i.e. radio, TV, print, billboards, and so on).

The Second Step Is Getting Visitors To Your Website.

Once you've been found by a prospective customer, no matter how it is that they found you, you need to get them to where they can get in touch with you and/or buy from you.

While there are many ways to increase traffic to a website, we'll focus on a few of the simplest and most effective ways. It's often faster to get found via sites or ads that link back to your site, such as YouTube, Google Ad Words, online press releases or Facebook. To get visitors from those sites to your site, first of all you need a link back to your site. Then you need to make it more compelling for the reader to click to, and visit, your site.

Let's say, for example, you use a video that gets you to the first page of Google. We've done this in less than an hour, though that depends on competition and other factors. You want to make sure to put a link to your website in the description, ideally on the first line so that it's visible without having to "read more". Be sure to use the http:// in front of the URL so that it converts into a link – you want to make it as easy as possible, every step of the way, for people to do business with you. If people have to copy and paste, some of them just won't make the effort, and you will have missed out on potential sales. You should also have a website address in the video itself.

What will work best for your business? That depends, and testing will reveal what really works best. But in general, having the link there and having a compelling call to action will mean that a certain percentage of visitors to that page will click through the link and visit your site. Once they're there, you have more control about how you can entice them to open their wallets in exchange for you providing something they will value enough to part with their hard-earned cash.

The Third Major Step Is To Increase Your Conversion Rate.

What's a conversion rate? That's the percentage of visitors who actually take an action that you want them to take – such as buying your products or services, signing up for your newsletter, sharing their page with your social networks, and so on. But to really increase your sales, let's focus on the first of those: buying.

So how exactly do you increase your conversion rate? Testing will truly tell what works for your particular business, but in general, there are several key elements that can have an impact on your sales. We'll go into more detail in a moment. Typically, the more benefit you can spell out, the more credibility you have and can show, and the more you can whet the customer's appetite for what you have to offer, the better your conversion rate will be.

Obviously it depends on what you have for sale – lower-priced items and more "impulse" purchases tend to convert better online with less effort. The buying decision for a simpler, lower-priced product tends to be faster and easier.

For higher-priced sales, the sales process tends to be more consultative. People have more questions about higher-priced or more complex items before they decide to buy. This also holds true for health-related products, especially things you would ingest, such as nutritional supplements.

A few general tips to increase your conversions are:

1) **Provide a lot of detail in the product description.** Images, videos, and text descriptions of the features all help. For products, different types of images may convert better than others. Let's take a book for example. Many studies have shown that having a 3D

image of a book (as opposed to a flat scan of the cover) can increase sales rather dramatically.

2) **Detail the benefits the buyer gets** when they open their wallet and buy your product. This is powerful – after all, most people buy based on the benefit of what they'll get – not just on the technical specs or a bland list of features. That said, it's important to include those details because they support the benefits. Plus, that can also help with your SEO efforts. People frequently search for a solution to a problem they're experiencing, and benefit descriptions should be worded as solutions to problems.

3) **Appeal to their emotions** – Sell the sizzle, not just the steak. Remember, facts tell, stories sell. A story about how someone benefitted from buying and using your product, told properly, can help the prospective buyer visualize themselves in the same situation and finding that the product would work for them, too.

4) **Have a "Buy Now" button**, "Add to Cart" button or something like that, and make it very easy to find. If you're using a long sales letter page, you may want to test having multiple "buy now" buttons scattered throughout the page. If you're really into the details of testing conversions, you'll want to use different codes for each button, so you can determine which button actually produced the most sales. You can also test different wording – "Buy Now" might convert better than "Add to Cart", or something else entirely different might be best.

5) **Tell them exactly how to buy** – in a video, you might say "Click the 'Buy Now' button below to get your ___ now." You might have a red arrow pointing to the button, or

some other way to highlight it and make it stand out from the rest of the page. In general, the more clearly you tell your prospective customers exactly what to do and how to buy, the more likely they will do so.

6) **Provide social proof.** In case you're not familiar with this concept, in general the more that people see others doing something, the more likely they are to do it as well. Here's an example: If you're in a strange town and deciding where to have dinner, and there are 2 restaurants to choose from, which do you choose? The one that's almost full or the one with only a couple of people? Most people would choose the busy restaurant because of social proof – if it's busy, other people must like it so it's probably better than the one that's not busy. Of course, there are other factors, but this is a basic psychological concept and all else being equal, strong social proof can influence the buying decision. When you use statistics, be sure to reference the source. If you just say that 9 out of 10 dentists prefer XYZ toothpaste, that's one thing. But including a reference to a study published in multiple scientific journals? That's much more powerful.

If you have client testimonials, endorsements, and so on – use them (but if you're in the U.S., make sure you abide by FTC guidelines). The more credible the testimonial, the better. In order of credibility from lowest to highest, here are some general types of testimonials:

    a. A written testimonial without a name
    b. A written testimonial with a name
    c. A written testimonial with a name and city
    d. A written testimonial with a picture

    e. A video testimonial

You can also embed third-party testimonials, such as those from Yelp!, Google, Citysearch, and more. Including LinkedIn recommendations with a link to the recommendation is also highly credible.

Adding logos such as the Better Business Bureau, reputable industry associations, links to press coverage, and online security companies can also help. For example, if you see that a site is verified "hacker safe" and is tested daily, you're probably going to be more comfortable entering your credit card info online than you might be otherwise.

I use this in my own business on my press page at **http://www.AtlantaSEOs.com/press**. I've taken this a step further and also included the most well-known logos right up at the top, then after that I have the links to each and every one in reverse chronological order all the way down the page.

There are other factors that can have an impact on your conversion rate, and you can get really granular with your testing. That's one of the key advantages to online marketing – you can measure impact at a really granular level and test even tiny variations easily. Things like color, fonts, backgrounds, website layout, and more can increase or decrease your sales.

We've touched on testing a lot, and this is crucial, but you can start by modeling what successful companies do. There are reasons why Amazon, Zappo's and other companies got to where they are today. And they have no doubt done a lot of testing as well. Like management guru Peter Drucker said, "what gets measured gets managed."

Now for a Bonus Tip: How To Continually Increase Your Sales

It's pretty simple, actually. Sell more to your customers and sell to them more often.

Sell more to your customers by increasing the average purchase price. Sell to them more often by encouraging them to come back again and again – give them incentives to come back.

Offer upsells, downsells, cross-sales, one-time-offers and so on. A customer tends to be most likely to spend more money when they already have their wallet in hand. You'll have to test what works best for your business, but try making additional offers once they've decided to buy. Amazon.com is great at this – they and many other sites use a recommendation engine to suggest other items that others who bought what you're buying also bought. Directly related items and accessories also tend to convert at higher rates. Just like in a department store where a good salesperson would offer to sell you a shirt and tie that matches that new suit, or the "would you like fries with that?" question that grew McDonald's sales significantly, selling more to the same customer is a powerful way to grow your sales.

Get customers and prospects on your email list so you can market to them more often. This can be as simple as having a signup form on each page of your website. Grow your list faster by offering something of value to encourage signups – people don't want to get on yet another email list these days – you've got to give them some incentive. That may be a free product, coupons and discounts, trial offer, white paper, special report, mini-course or something else… get creative and think about it from the customer's viewpoint. What would be helpful for them? If you're a restaurant, you might offer a free appetizer, meal or a drawing for dinner for two. If you're a doctor, you might give away a free examination. A car dealership might offer a free oil change or detailing. Get creative – there are lots of ways to add value, many at no additional cost to you. You can also use these kinds of "ethical bribes" to grow your fan base on Facebook and increase your reach across other social networks.

Sometimes there is a line between marketing enough to satisfy people's needs and marketing too often and alienating your subscribers. So pay attention to not only sales figures, but also decreases in subscribers, drops in social media activity and other indicators.

About David B. Wright

David B. Wright is a top-ranking author and is President & Chief Marketing Officer of W3 Group, a marketing firm that helps businesses get more business. David provides marketing services ranging from high-level strategic direction down to the tactical implementation including SEO, mobile, local, social, video marketing, online PR, and more. David has done business around the world and has been quoted in numerous publications, including Inc. Magazine, The Wall Street Journal, CNN, AMEX Open Forum, About.com, and Business Insider.

David B. Wright
Chief Marketing Officer

Cell: **770-490-3950**
Google Voice: **404-669-6682**
eFax: **208-545-1241**

http://www.AtlantaSEOs.com/press
http://www.GetAJobBook.com

Chapter 5
Keys to Marketing In A Pressed Economy
By James Sheets

It was the best of times, it was the worst of times, it was the age of wisdom, it was the age of foolishness, it was the epoch of belief, it was the epoch of incredulity, it was the season of Light, it was the season of Darkness, it was the spring of hope, it was the winter of despair, we had everything before us, we had nothing before us, we were all going direct to heaven, we were all going direct the other way - in short, the period was so far like the present period, that some of its noisiest authorities insisted on its being received, for good or for evil, in the superlative degree of comparison only.
– Charles Dickens in A Tale of Two Cities

Dickens' words ring down through the corridors of time as apropos as ever – we are not in Kansas anymore, Toto! The old tried, true and trusted paths that almost "guaranteed" small business success and profitability aren't quite as reliable as they used to be. Times have changed, marketing tools have changed, and marketing strategies have to change as well if you are to compete in the "new day" we find ourselves in.

The "anything goes" and "we will still make money" era of the eighties and nineties have given way to the "I don't just want it to work, it HAS to work" era. As an American small business owner you find placed solidly between the "rock" of a suppressed economy and the "hard place" of an almost universal fear of failure. And if I were a betting man, I would wager that you are tempted to do the absolute worst thing that you could ever do at a time like this – and that is to cut back on the only thing that can help you ride out the storm and come out on the other side solvent and still in the race – an effective marketing strategy and a strong marketing budget.

LEARNING FROM HISTORY

If you look back over the last one hundred years in our country, one of the prominent things that stands out about the businesses that survived turbulent economic challenges is they continued "against all odds" to invest in a marketing strategy that "paid off" in eventual growth in their businesses, while all around them "wise" entrepreneurs reduced or did away with their marketing budget, and therefore experienced a continuous decrease in sales.

The question that should be at the forefront of your mind then is: how do I successfully market during a recession? The good news is there are several low-cost and even no-cost ways you can market your products and/or services that will enable you to both sustain your business presence, and to do so profitably - even in the midst of difficult financial times.

The first thing you must commit to is: Don't you even dare think about cutting your marketing budget! If you ever hope to see results, now is not just the time to work harder, it is the time to work smarter, especially in regards to your marketing dollars. Now, more than ever, we must exercise what I call customer intelligence.

KNOW YOUR CUSTOMERS

Let me encourage you to start viewing your marketing budget as an investment and not an expense. Develop a marketing strategy and push forward. Small and mid-size business leaders with a clear marketing vision survive difficult financial times and come out on the other side strong.

A Couple Of Success Strategies That Can Empower And Position You For Success:

KNOW YOUR CONSUMER

Identify who they are, where they are and how they think. Find out how the economy is affecting them, and then market your message about your product or service around their pain. Feel their pain and reach out to them with an authentic desire to help them succeed. This might require a rethinking and revising of a business' product line or service, but the resultant payoff will more than compensate the time, effort and money involved. You have to be open to considering how to develop lower cost solutions if possible. They must be flexible, but at the same time be cognizant and discerning.

WHICH WAY DID THEY GO?

Do you know how you can identify small businesses? They think like small businesses. Do you know how you can recognize small businesses that are destined for growth? They refuse to think and strategize like a small business! If you cut your marketing budget, how will new customers find you? Whenever a small business cuts its marketing budget, they have effectively severed their business lifeline and greatly reduced any legitimate hope of potential growth. Success can happen; it can be achieved, but realistically not without a marketing plan.

FIND THE EYES OF YOUR CUSTOMERS

In today's business market it is difficult to get the attention of your consumer. Over the last few weeks and months I have spoken to several business owners that have said they recognize the importance of marketing but now wasn't the time for them to invest in marketing their business, maybe later. In other words, after I am successful I will do the things that will make me successful! The sad thing is that often when I come back by to check in on them later, many have went out of business. And you can bet your bottom dollar that one of the contributing factors is that they pulled their marketing budget!

THE BIG THREE AREAS OF CHANGE TO BE AWARE OF

Anytime there is a repressed economy it will almost always result in three areas being affected:
- Budget Modifications
- Consumer Buying Behavior
- Taking Advantage of Market opportunity

IMPLEMENT APPROPRIATE BUDGET MODIFICATIONS

When it comes to budget modifications, small businesses typically make the mistake of reducing their marketing budget.

As I said earlier, the fact is that by doing this, they are effectively reducing their product/service communications which not only affects short term sales, it also negatively affects the long-term bottom line – profit!

While reducing the marketing budget might offer short-term relief, to achieve that you have to risk losing increased market share once the economy eventually begins to stabilize and recovery begins. Instead of reducing your marketing budget, let me encourage you to look for effective ways to be more cost efficient rather than committing business suicide by reducing budgets.

DISCOVER THE CURRENT CONSUMER BUYING BEHAVIOR

It is no secret that during times of recession, consumer behavior changes, and that can naturally affects a business' bottom line. During recessions, people tend to spend less and delay, or even put off major purchases. But look around, not all consumers have stopped spending money. People sometimes change their buying habits based on their immediate financial situations, but you can bet your bottom dollar (pun intended), they will never stop spending. They may purchase less expensive brands or alternative products during slow economic times, but if your business maintains brand and customer loyalty, when the economy begins recovery, your customers will be more than happy to return to the more desirable brands or services they prefer.

That is why it is so important that you continue to place your products and services before your present (and potential) customers. A strong marketing strategy positions customers and helps them justify, and thus stimulate, a purchase. Remember most purchases are emotional, not intellectual. So if you are committed to developing a lower cost solution, this helps position you with your customers, even through difficult times. This will help you keep your customers loyal, and help to cultivate a strong relationship for the future.

Have you noticed that the majority of successful businesses continue to advertise during times of recession and thus continue to see strong sales and revenue? Smart businesses do not rely solely on price cutting; instead, they work to develop creative alternatives that fit in line with the consumers' desires and budget. In today's market, consumers are looking for loyalty, not a one-night stand. The question you must ask is: are you providing a loyalty building solution for your customers during this difficult time?

TAKING ADVANTAGE OF MARKET OPPORTUNITY

A fact of life – markets change, resulting in the need for creatively taking advantage of market opportunities. There will be price wars; there will be stronger competition and possibly less money in the market. But these liabilities co-exist with opportunities as well. One of the givens is during recessions media revenue often deflates – which sometimes mean it might be a good time to make your product or service known without high media expenditure. On the other hand, while your competition is cutting their budgets, resulting in reduced activity, perhaps it's time for you to take yours up a notch and gain a larger market share. Sometimes the price is right.

FOLLOW THE YELLOW BRICK ROAD

Many business owners I speak with are at a disadvantage because they know their product or service, but they don't know effective ways to market. They are looking for effective ways to market that doesn't cost an arm and a leg. In other words, how can you get the word out without driving your company into the deep, dark financial black hole?

It is true that marketing takes money, but thankfully there are effective low-cost, and even some no-cost options that when put into action can help get the word out about your products and services. But let me give you a heads up: nothing is free. While some of the free, or no-cost ideas may not cost you lots of money, they will cost you time, so be prepared for that.

Let me share a couple effective ways – that really work - that your company can start using right away. You don't have to use them all; choose one or two and get to work – this week! Once you begin to see these marketing strategies begin to work for you, wild bulls will not be able to stop you from riding the crest of the momentum you have started.

NETWORK AT EVENTS

Don't just belong to the local Chamber of Commerce meetings, attend them. There are also BNI Group meetings, and other business oriented meetings that are attended by your "ideal" clients. Collect business cards (everyone will be glad to give you a couple). Take them back home and then begin to make phone calls and send out emails to follow up. One warning - do this immediately while you're meeting with them while this is still fresh in their minds. Important: if they don't immediately require your services, ask them if they know of someone who can, and get their contact information.

FORMULATE AN ELEVATOR SPEECH.

Create a 30 or 60 second sound bite that will catch the attention of people you meet and cause you to stand out from everyone else. Many people talk to hear their head rattle, or only to "make a sell", but when you can share who you are and what you do, or how you can help them solve a problem – they want to know more about you!

CREATE JOINT-VENTURES.

Look for and set up meetings with other business leaders whose products or services compliment yours, and do joint promotions. For example, I do joint-ventures with copywriters and graphic designers. Who would be a good candidate for a joint-venture with you?

CONTACT THE EDITORS OF LOCAL NEWSPAPERS

They are always looking for interesting and newsworthy items to write about, especially if they involve local people or businesses. And you will be pleasantly surprised how effective an article about your business, product or service can be.

Just implementing one of these ideas on a weekly basis can make a significant impact in your business within one month. See you in the winner's circle!

About James Sheets

James Sheets was listed in Who's Who Among American High School Students, has a Theology degree from Adonai Christian International University, has served for over 34 years in the capacity of pastor, teacher, evangelist, counselor, author, songwriter, worship leader, missionary, life coach, and mentor to other spiritual leaders. James believes in giving back from the overflow of what he has received, so he started Basileia Marketing and Media, where he helps entrepreneurs, business owners and non-profits brand themselves, and market their brand. James lives in Stockbridge, Georgia with his lovely wife, Dr. Kaye Sheets

Jwsheets@comf5.com

Chapter 6

Discover the 3 Secrets Most Entrepreneurs Will Never Know About Becoming Successful

By Danette Moss

"People have to get to know you in order to feel comfortable with who you are and what you do."
-Danette Moss, Small Business Strategist

Many business professionals will tell you that more is better. As a matter of fact, what they are REALLY saying is that since they don't have a targeted approach to selling, that they are using the shot gun approach to gaining customers. However, in order for a marksman to hit a target, they have to be aiming at something in particular.

"Let's Talk Strategies" with Danette Moss was birthed out of making sure that people got educated and that they got the things they needed to be successful in business. Even if I couldn't give it to them I figured I'd give it to them by way of inviting people to the show; you know, inviting people that have those key things that my listening audience needed, and positioning myself as an expert as one that knows how to go and get the information that we truly need.

When it comes to running a successful online business, there are many places people turn to. Coming from a background in the concierge and errand service industry, I turned to Guy Kawasaki, former chief evangelist of Apple, Co-founder of

Alltop.com, founding partner of Garage Technology Ventures, and Author of the book's "The Art of the State", "Reality Check", and "Enchantment: The Art of Changing Hearts, Minds, and Actions".

If you are a solopreneur, entrepreneur or small business owner, you know there are a LOT of mistakes you can – and will – make. I thought I would share 3 things I have learned from Guy Kawasaki that have helped me to become a better business strategist and run my own successful online business and radio talk show. In his book "Enchantment: The Art of Changing Hearts, Minds, and Actions", he explains what enchantment is, when and why you need it, and the ethics of enchanting people.

What Is Enchantment?
(Source: Enchantment: The Art of Changing Hearts, Minds, and Actions)

When Karin Muller, filmmaker and author, was in the Peace Corps from 1987 to 1989, she dug wells and built schools in a village in the Philippines. One night, seventeen members of the New People's Army (NPA), the armed wing of the Communist Party of the Philippines, came to her (she knew that this was going to happen) so she collected two precious commodities: sugar and coffee.

When the NPA arrived, she exclaimed, "Thank God you're here. I've been waiting all day. Please have some coffee. Leave your guns at the door." Her reaction baffled the leader of the group, but he took off his gun and sat down for a cup of coffee. She avoided an interrogation or something worse because, according to Muller, "You can't interrogate someone you're having coffee with."

Muller did not react with anger, indignation, or panic (which is how I would have reacted). Instead, she touched an emotion in the leader of the group and transformed the situation from brute force and intimidation to conversation and communication. She delighted him with her unexpected hospitality and changed his heart, his mind, and his actions.

In short, she enchanted him. Enchantment can occur in villages, stores, dealerships, offices, boardrooms, and on the Internet. It is more than manipulating people to help get your way. Enchantment transforms situations and relationships. It converts hostility into civility. It reshapes civility into affinity. It changes skeptics and cynics into believers.

Take these 3 secrets, start applying them to your business just as I did, and watch your business explode.

Secret 1: When Is Enchantment Necessary?
Secret 2: Understanding What Potential Customers Are
          Thinking
Secret 3: Where Should You Draw the Line?

> *You have first to experience what you want to express.*
> *-Vincent van Gogh*

Secret 1: *When Is Enchantment Necessary?*

There are many tried-and-true methods to make a buck.

Enchantment is on a different curve: When you enchant people, your goal is not to make as much money as you can from them or to get them to do what you want, but to fill them with great delight.

Here are situations when you need enchantment the most:

- **Aspiring to lofty, idealistic results.** Want to change the world? Change caterpillars into butterflies? This takes more than run-of-the-mill relationships. You need to convince people to dream the same dream that you do.

- **Making difficult, infrequent decisions on purchasing your product or service.** The greater the difficulty of the product or service you're offering, the greater the need for enchantment. Factors that cause friction include cost, risk, and politics. If the purchase or your product or service is a big deal, then it's a big deal to make it happen.

- **Overcoming entrenched habits.** Most of the time, habits simplify life and enable fast, safe, and good decisions that can also prevent the adoption of a new idea. Enchantment can open the door for your potential customer to consider a decision.

- **Defying a crowd.** Following the crowd (just because all the gurus are doing it, doesn't mean you need to) isn't always wise. It can lead you down a path of destruction. People can tell when you've bit off more than you can chew. Stick to what you're good at and outsource the rest.

- **Proceeding despite delayed or nonexistent feedback.** Tenacity and dedication is necessary when feedback is rare or not readily available, and your efforts take a long time to see results. Sometimes the potential customer may not have it in their company or individual budget to make a decision right away. In these cases, moderate interest and support aren't enough.

Do any of these situations sound familiar to you? They should, because they are present whenever people have to make decisions about the purchase of a product or service that will affect their business.

> *Every sale has five basic obstacles:*
> *no need, no money, no trust.*
> *-Zig Ziglar*

Secret 2: *Understand What Your Potential Customers Are Thinking*

It doesn't matter how enchanted you are about your own products or services, or how many people you tell about it if you don't understand why everyone else does not feel the same way.

When it comes to your business one must understand what people are thinking, feeling, and believing in order to enchant them. If you fail there (which most entrepreneurs do) your business will never attract the customers needed to keep the doors open.

Image yourself as the person you want to enchant, and then ask yourself the following questions. If you can't honestly come up with a reasonable answer, don't expect your enchantment to work:

- What does this person want? You can't blame someone for wondering what your motives are. I'm not saying you should not benefit, but you should disclose your motivation to put the potential customer at ease.

- Is this product or service worth the investment? The next step is to help the potential customer understand how your cause ties into what they want. The benefits of the product or service must outweigh the cost of it as well as the benefits of not moving forward with using your products or services. The fact that you think your products or services are worthwhile is not enough; the person you're trying to enchant must believe this, too.
- Can I take the leap? Even if the products or services are worthwhile, can the potential customer do it? Factors that prevent the change include the expense, effort, and risk that your product or service requires. If the potential customer doubts they can be successful after using your products or services, even if they want to and believes, it's worth it.

It can take weeks, months or sometimes years for enchantment to occur, so prepare for a marathon, not a sprint. By doing this you create trust, other people will talk about you, and you will get more exposure, and those potential customers will not only become customers, but repeat customers.

Behavioral psychology is the science of
pulling habits out of rats.

-Douglas Busch

Secret 3: *Where Should You Draw the Line?*

Enchantment is not about getting your way solely for your own benefit. To the contrary, for enchantment to last, other people must benefit. A bright line must also be drawn between ethical and unethical activities. Do a check-up from the neck up to determine which side of the line you're on:

- **Are you asking people to do something that you wouldn't do?** If you won't do something, don't ask your potential customers to do it. Asking people to do what you would not do is manipulation, not enchantment, and it never works in the long run.

- **Do your interests conflict?** Enchantment endures if your interests are aligned with the interests of the potential customer. Alignment makes enchantment both ethical and more enjoyable. If the products or services you're providing to the potential customer (target audience/market) aren't aligned, you should either alter your product or services, or rethink your intended market.

- **Have you hidden any conflicts of interest?** Even if the interests of your product or service are aligned - according to you, you should disclose it. There is no such thing as too much disclosure.

- **Are you telling little "white lies"?** The slope is slippery when the big picture, or the greater good, seems to justify the means. There is no such thing, however, as a little "white lie". There are lies and truths, and nothing in between.

- **Are you enchanting gullible people?** Enchanting people who don't have the ability to discern if your product or service is good for them is flat out immoral. Although fooling gullible people happens every day, don't mistake this as success. It will only give you a false sense of competence that will eventually have you found out.

If you answered 'yes', or are struggling with some of these questions, I encourage you to make a change immediately as it will eventually catch up to you. Go ahead - improve your skills by transforming your enchantment today.

If your business involves service of any kind, tune into "Let's Talk Strategies" with Danette Moss and listen in to the conversations I have with millionaires and highly successful entrepreneurs highlighting topics on Social Media, Business Strategies, Networking, Internet Marketing and Business Processes that benefit small business owners. You are sure to learn ways to implement online business strategies and tools that will explode your potential for success!

My motto: "Work to live. Don't live to work."

"Let's Talk Strategies" helps you identify where you are and craft an action plan to utilize time, people and resources to get you to where you want to go next.

About Danette Moss

Danette Moss, is a small business strategist, information marketer, coach and author of the book **Let's Talk Strategies: Conversations with Millionaires and Highly Successful Entrepreneurs, The Solopreneurs Guide to Success**. She is the host of a weekly Blog Talk Radio Show – "Let's Talk Strategies" that highlights topics on Social Media, Business Strategies, Networking, Internet Marketing and Business Processes that benefit small business owners. Danette's mission is to help those that are stuck move forward in owning and operating successful businesses. WordPress training, automating your business, information marketing, business coaching, and social networking are some of the many services Danette provides.

In 2001 while working at night in the IT Field, Danette's stress load became overwhelming, which lead her to find something unique and different to do. Family members and friends were requesting her services to make reservations and run errands for them when she in fact should have been "sleeping". The thought came that she should create a business of this and charge people. She started her research, and after being displaced from that field she whole heartedly persuaded her new dream. Danette says she wouldn't trade this venture for the world. This new endeavour allows her the flexibility to spend time with her retired husband, 5 children, and 3 grandchildren.

Danette, whose reputation is highly regarded in her area, was asked by a company which manages upscale apartment communities to revamp their entire concierge system. In addition, she has offered her services to major companies located within the tenant area of Atlanta Marriott Marquis. She operated a call center for Sophia's Shopping Service for several years, and eventually took over their entire list of residential and corporate clients in 2008.

She was a guest speaker two years in a row at the Annual ICEA Conference and plans to use her expertise to empower hundreds of concierge and errand owners to reach new levels of professional excellence. Danette contributes her success to her integrity, tenacity, and her commitment to exceptional customer service. She has devoted herself to educating solopreneurs/small business owners by equipping them with the necessary skills and steps to succeed in the service industry.

For bookings and more:

    Let's Talk Strategies
    931 Monroe Drive
    Suite A-102, #425
    Atlanta, GA 30308
    Contact: 404.482.2546
    Email: **info@letstalkstrategies.com**

Chapter 7
How To Use Authentic Marketing & Sales To Attract Your Ideal Clients And Make More Profits!
By Diane Conklin

Is There A Difference Between Marketing And Sales?

One of the first concerns many new business owners and entrepreneurs have is they don't like the thought of selling things. Sales is a dirty word for most people, but if you think about it, you'll realize nobody makes any money in the world without somebody buying something...or without something being sold.

A tank of gas to fill up your car, a movie ticket to see the hot new movie that's out right now, a new pair of running shoes, groceries so you can eat, all of these are examples of things we buy, but don't really feel like we've been "sold" something when we spend money on these things.

The real issue isn't that people don't want to buy; it's that nobody likes to be sold. Everyone likes to buy. And, with the right marketing, with the right product or service to the right people, they will buy and buy and buy. And, you'll make money when they do, because you're providing them a quality product or service – and you both feel good about it.

It's a win, win, win situation! And, that's what marketing and sales are all about - everyone feeling like they walked away from the situation a winner and further ahead than where they were when they started the interaction with you.

So, yes, there's a difference between sales and marketing. One good definition of marketing is everything you do to create, or put yourself in sales situations. In other words, marketing is anything and everything you do to create an opportunity, and a desire, for a prospect or client, to buy your products and services.

Sales, on the other hand, is about getting either face-to-face with the prospect, or in front of a group of prospects. This is where the money is actually exchanged. Sales can be made through a sales letter, by getting one-on-one with the prospect (but don't worry, this isn't the way you'll be selling), from the platform, or on a teleseminar or webinar, just to name a few.

Sales are really about helping people solve their problems. It's providing solutions for people and getting paid to do it. Sales, done right is always a win-win situation. That's the kind of sales all of us want to be involved in.

Why Is Marketing So Important?

Marketing is the most important thing you'll do in your business. Using sound marketing principles, strategies and techniques will allow you to build a large list, form great relationships with your prospects and clients, and provide them with outstanding products and services, that they want, get value from, and that you're proud of.

The marketer always wins, because as a great marketer, you always have the ability to make money, no matter what the economy is doing, whether the housing market is going up or down, when the stock market is soaring or when it's crashing.

None of that will matter to you. If you learn good marketing techniques and put them to work in your business, you will be a success.

Direct Response Marketing and Your Money

Once you have qualified prospects that have an interest in your products and services, how do you convert those qualified leads and prospects into buying customers, clients and raving fans? You do it with good, solid marketing strategies, by under promising and over delivering, by providing good content, following up, and by continuing to market and sell to these people over and over again.

You're going to get your best marketing results and make the most money by using Direct Response Marketing strategies and techniques. Direct Response Marketing is not the type of advertising you typically see on TV, in newspapers and magazines, or anywhere else.

That's what's called image advertising, and it's what all the big companies use. Companies like Coca-Cola, IBM, Apple, Nike, and all the others use image advertising. These companies have millions of dollars to spend to get their names out to you, and they do it so many times, over and over again, that's what they bank on – you remembering their name over somebody else's.

That's not the kind of marketing you want to do to grow your business – as a small business owner, you can't compete with the big boys, so don't even try. Most small business owners don't have millions of dollars to put into a Super Bowl ad or have the time or money to invest millions on televisions ads, thousands on newspaper ads, or to compete in that arena.

Small business owners have to invest smart in their marketing, doing things that are measureable, so they know where their marketing dollars are working the best, and then make smart decisions about where to invest more and where to pull back. That's exactly where direct response marketing strategies come into play.

In your local area, you don't have to look any further than the Yellow Pages to see image advertising. The ads all look alike – that's called "me too advertising". You just do the exact same thing everybody else is doing. It must work if everybody's doing it, right? Wrong! It's likely that none of them are measuring their results, so they don't know if their ads are working or not.

All those advertisers have businesses, but they don't know what to do, so they do what the sales rep tells them to do, which is put a typical ad in there with your company name, location, hours of operation and your phone number. If you're lucky, they will include a website and maybe some social media references as well.

The Direct Response Marketer asks this question about any ad they place anywhere, and any marketing they do – "How will I know how much business I get from this ad?" Then, you place some type of measuring devise on the ad. For example, in this example, you could make an offer of 10% off when they bring the coupon attached to your ad into the store, you could offer them a free report by calling your special 800 number (which is set up solely to measure how many calls you get from that one ad) or a host of other ideas. The point is, again, you must be able to measure the response from that specific media, that specific campaign, and that specific ad.

Use marketing methods that are measureable, where you quickly know whether your efforts and money are pulling in a return or not. If they're producing good results, you roll out the plan and do more; if they aren't, you stop and regroup – quickly, so you can make a lot of money in a short period of time.

Direct Response Marketing is the kind of marketing you do if you want fast, trackable results from your marketing. It's the kind of marketing where you can spend $1.00 and get back $10.00, do it quickly, over and over again, and know what your results are within a few days, hours, or minutes – depending on what media you use to market your product.

If you use traditional image advertising methods, you'll never be able to measure the return on your marketing dollars. There will be no way to measure it, because you won't know where your clients are coming from. You just keep spending money on marketing, hoping it's working. If you place the typical image ad, with no measuring device, you could be wasting thousands of dollars every year, with no return on your investment, and not even know it.

Authentic Marketing And Persuasion

Marketing is about building relationships that lead to sales. Sometimes this happens relatively quickly and sometimes it takes a little longer to develop. Good, authentic marketing is always about building long term relationships.

Good marketing is never about manipulation. Good marketing many times involves persuasion.

The difference between manipulation and persuasion is simple. Manipulation is about getting somebody to do something that benefits you, and persuasion is convincing that person to do something that benefits them.

If you're truly solving a problem or providing a good solution to another person who is in need of that product or service at that time, then there is never any manipulation involved in the process. There simply can't be because you are simply fulfilling a need.

Being a good marketer, not necessarily a great one, being consistent, and converting your marketing to sales will bring you a great deal of success in your business, no matter what you do or what media you use to market (and you should be using multiple media and integrating your marketing).

Add to this a good marketing Plan, Leverage your business with team, technology and other factors, take massive, focused Action, always looking at what's Next in your business along with what you're doing Now, and use good solid Strategy and Systems, and you will have a thriving business that will provide you and many others with whatever your goals are...for you and the world - as your R.I.P.P.L.E.S. (Repetition In Place Produces Little Effects Somewhere) expand throughout the world, as you provide service and contribution.

And, remember, It Doesn't Have To Be So Hard!

About Diane Conklin

Diane Conklin is an internationally known author, entrepreneur, coach, consultant, event planner, speaker and copywriter. Diane is a direct response marketing expert who specializes in showing small business owners how to integrate their online and offline marketing strategies, media and methods, to get maximum results from their marketing dollars.

As a marketing and business strategist, Diane shows entrepreneurs and small business owners how to outperform their competition by measuring their marketing, and strategically use multi-media campaigns to stand alone in their marketplace as the go-to provider for their products and services.

She is the founder of Complete Marketing Systems, and for more than 14 years has been showing small business owners how to start, build, and grow businesses, where they take knowledge they already possess and turn it into passive, ongoing, leveraged profits.

Diane routinely helps small business owners take their businesses to the next level, whether they're just starting out and want to quickly grow to six figures, or if they already have an established business and want to take it to seven figures and beyond.

As a business and marketing strategist, Diane has been involved in numerous campaigns grossing over $1,000,000.00 in sales several times in her career.

Diane has proprietary home study systems, coaching programs, masterminds, and provides done-for-you services in the areas of Social Media, Information Marketing, Direct Response Marketing, Direct Mail, and Event Marketing, Planning and Management.

As a speaker, Diane has shared the stage with the likes of Joan Rivers, George Foreman, Dan Kennedy, Bill Glazer, Harry Dent, Barbara Corcoran, James Malinchak, Peggy McColl, Brendon Burchard, Sandra Yancey and many others.

Diane was voted Marketer of the Year for her innovative marketing strategies and campaigns.

Diane Conklin

(866) 293-0589

www.CompleteMarketingSystems.com
www.Facebook.com/DianeConklinFan
www.Twitter.com/DianeConklin

Chapter 8
The Mastery Of A Joint Venture Broker
By Muhammad Siddique

The most important element of doing Joint Ventures, or JV's, is having the right JV Mindset. You'll find doing JV's without it tends to become quite frustrating. But with it, you'll enjoy the process and the fruits of your labor.

Mindset is very important in this business. If you don't have the mindset of success, then you're destined to fail. Therefore, you need to understand the Law of Attraction, and utilize it to enable your mind, body and spirit to work in harmony for attracting and manifesting your desires and goals.

Anyone is capable of success if they put their mind to it, believe in themselves and take action to make it happen – even YOU! The Law of Attraction, when properly utilized, helps enable you with the proper mindset and strategies you desire.

Visualization is probably the best means of manifesting something specific using the Law of Attraction. In general, however, you may wish to generate a type of energy around yourself to continually be attracting certain energies that will serve you. For example, using affirmations can be very effective.

If you want to attract the energy of opportunity, then you could use an affirmation such as "I am the right person, in the right place, at the right time, doing the right things, with the right people!" This is a great one for manifesting beneficial joint ventures and joint venture partners.

If you want to attract joint venture opportunities specifically, you could use an affirmation such as "I am aware of and open to unlimited joint venture opportunities; I am involved in the best 'high-level' joint venture opportunities".

When you start doing deals, it is vitally important you start seeing yourself as someone who is on a mission to add value. You want to help others. You know exactly what your partners need, you know full well what would be of benefit to their clients, and you make it happen.

If you want them to feel something, you must feel it on a very deep level first. If you want them to see you as an expert, you must first see yourself as an expert. If you live it, breathe it and project it, doors will open and you will start seeing impressive results!

The Role Of The JV Broker

The role of the JV broker is a person who finds JV partners, sets up the deal and takes a percentage of the profits. You can make a lot of money by simply being a middleman or JV broker.

JV brokering is not a very difficult concept to understand. Just imagine an orchestra. Surely, such an ensemble wouldn't be able to play marvelous music without the help of a conductor. The conductor simply brings all the band members together and commands them how to proceed with a masterpiece. The conductor doesn't have to play any musical instruments; he just needs a good working knowledge.

The appeal of JV brokering lies in the fact that you can actually earn really good money by being one without having to create your own product, without having to employ any marketing strategies, and more often than not, without having to invest anything financially.

The JV broker essentially determines the type of resources the client needs, and works with the client to determine what can be offered to joint venture partners.

The JV broker also works out how to present the offer to joint venture partners where the prospective partners see the win-win situation.

Approaching potential JV partners in just the right way is vital to the outcome of the joint venture. The JV broker's role will be to assist the client when trying to convince people who have never heard of the client to enter into a JV deal through a well crafted JV proposal.

The JV broker has already determined what a potential JV partner can gain for the deal. They've done their research, they know who needs what resources, and they know how to find others to provide those resources.

I always tell people who ask me about JV brokering that in order to be a successful JV broker, a person MUST possess the following:

- A creative mindset
- A comprehensive and diverse network of contacts
- A good knowledge of your industry
- Good communication and negotiating skills
- A will to succeed

I can teach you the above, except however, the will to succeed. This needs to come from within you. Anyone else can try their best to bring out the competitive fire within you, but you alone must be able to conjure that fire and use it to your advantage.

Other roles of a JV broker include:
- Planning the joint venture
- Managing the complete joint venture
- Day to day operation, support and advice on the joint venture
- Reviewing terms of service
- Consulting with clients on joint venture partners
- Locating, analyzing and recruiting top producing joint venture partners
- Screening, reviewing and approving potential joint venture partners
- Monitoring and motivating underperforming joint venture partners
- Working with joint venture partners on improving conversions
- Reporting Issues and resolving potential problems
- Reviewing and assessing products/services from a marketing perspective

- Maintaining contact with joint venture partners, handling all emails/calls

The Benefits Of Being A JV Broker

JV Brokering is such a lucrative and exclusive field. Knowing all the advantages you can derive in a career as a JV broker will develop within you a love for this job like I have. Loving your work is essential to your success, of course.

JV brokering, you see, is a highly creative business. It may not seem apparent right now, but trust me, there is more creativity involved in JV brokering than in any other field of marketing.

Let's look at some of the benefits that can be brought about by being a JV broker:

- You don't need to spend years building your customer list and constantly trying to build a better relationship with your subscriber base.
- You don't need to keep track of the sales made, of how much money is owed to whom, of fulfilling the product and sending it out, etc.
- You just step in, leverage those resources, and make colossal profits by bringing people together and contributing to others.
- You will be known as an expert that makes things happen and more opportunities will fall in your lap.
- As a JV broker your market is not seasonal in nature. Demand for your services runs the whole duration of each and every passing year.

- There will always be a need for a JV broker. For as long as businesses seek out fresh ideas to expand their enterprises and increase their profits, and seek out other businesses that compliment theirs, a JV broker will always be in demand.

Not only is JV brokering a great way of earning a fantastic living, it is also a marvelous way of positioning yourself as an established personality in the marketing field.

As a JV broker I have been approached by some of the biggest business gurus in the world to help them find JV partners, and also work on some lucrative joint venture projects just because there are not many JV experts available!

Imagine… if like me you're able to broker a gigantic deal that revolutionizes the industry because of its sheer expanse and the imagination that inspired it, you will forever be known as the mind that authored the project that people talk about for many years – you may even be invited to speak at some very 'high-profile' events worldwide like I do!

Muhammad Siddique

Muhammad Siddique a.k.a Siddique is a Joint Venture Broker, B2B Sales Lead Generation Expert and Linkedin Strategist who produces results for B2B clients on harnessing social media and the digital space to bring brand awareness directly to businesses.

His work includes being a joint venture broker, marketing on Linkedin, Twitter, Facebook, Youtube and hundreds of other social media sites.

His core expertise includes:

- Joint Venture Brokering

- B2B Sales Lead Generation

- B2B Linkedin Marketing

- Social Media Lead Generation

- Social Networks & Joint Ventures

- Social Media Strategies

- Video Marketing

- Online Reputation Management

- Brand Management on social Media

- Social Media Campaign Management

- Local Marketing

Siddique partners with companies and creates new ways to grow revenues by leveraging hidden assets you have and you do not even know about.

siddique@trcb.com

skype id: siddique30024

http://facebook.com/siddiquefans

Chapter 9

Wake the F#¢% Up … It's NOT Working!
Architect Your Business to Support your Life
By David Taylor-Klaus

It's Not Working

I sleepwalked through the first few acts of my adult life. When the fog *lifted* – thanks to a series of fortunate events -- I looked around at my life. I didn't like what I saw. Something had to change.

To the outside world, everything looked great. I had been married for a dozen years (to a woman I'd known since age 11), and had 3 kids who were all in private school. I had a 10 year old Internet business and a pretty good reputation in the industry. My wine cellar was full, and I had just medaled, rowing in the Georgia State Games.

I was going through the motions of a wonderful life. But I was hollow inside. My life just wasn't working.

At some point, when you won't slow down on your own, God, the Universe, whatever you want to call it will thwack you on the back of the head and get your attention.

I got my wake-up call at 39.

It wasn't a heart-attack, or cancer, or a divorce, or anything similarly catastrophic. I was damn lucky, really. I got sick. Really sick. I got better. And then, I started over.

It wasn't like I turned on a dime. There were gradual changes that led to that wake-up call. But once I became aware, there was no turning back.

I had been moving full steam ahead for over a decade with no clear direction, never slowing down enough to set a destination. What success I had came from being reactive, rather than pro-active. I wasn't participating consciously as a husband, father, business partner, or entrepreneur.

Each day, as I climbed the stairs to my office, my stomach turned. I was uninspired by the work we were doing, the people who were working for us, and the role I was playing. My business partner and I weren't having the conversations we needed to have, and we weren't taking the actions we needed to take. I was wearing myself out, trying to "get it all done," desperate to **feel** successful – somewhere!

But you can't be inspirational from a place of desperation, and when an entrepreneur lacks inspiration and passion, everything is flat – professionally and personally.

I had no driving purpose. It's like I was never really present – anywhere. I got so consumed by everything that was going on that I wasn't being intentional about anything in particular. I was going through the motions day to day, trying to fulfill the responsibilities of each of my roles, but none of them with a clear sense of what Simon Sinek calls my "why."

Marshall Goldsmith said in his Mindful Leadership presentation for Leaders@Google, "Truly successful people have mojo.

They're finding happiness and meaning in what they're doing now. That, to me, is the definition of success."

I was working hard, but Goldsmith's vision of success was eluding me.

I knew there was something more. I was convinced that there was something better. And I was ready to change. I was no longer willing to tolerate sleep walking through my life.

We Have It Backwards

In retrospect, I can see clearly why I was lost, and what it took for me to recover. I see the 5 steps that are necessary to reclaim a sense of meaning and purpose, and the over-arching role that vision plays in making it possible. Now, I have the privilege of working with others to rediscover themselves, their families and their reason for being. As I said, I have been damn lucky.

I've come to realize that too many of us forge ahead through life, using everyone else's yardstick to determine success. We pursue our careers, and try to fit our lives into the remaining spaces.

We have it backwards.

James Campbell Quick, a professor of organizational behavior at the University of Texas-Arlington captures the current cultural ethos: "to get ahead, a 70 hour work week is the new standard. What little time is left is often divvied up among relationships, kids and sleep."

When considering balance, it has become the cultural norm to put "work" first in the balance equation. In a Google search for *life-work balance* (notice the word order), 75 of the first 100 results were for *work-life balance, work-work balance* and *work-life-work balance.*

We have it backwards.

I no longer accept: "that's just the way it is." Since I woke up, and took a leadership position in my own life, I am no longer okay with people going through the motions without a clear sense of purpose. Yes, I am intolerant. Yes, I stand in judgment. And my work helps people create the kind of Life-Work Balance that produces profitable businesses, and thriving families.

5 Steps to Life-Work Balance

There are 5 steps to truly achieve Life-Work Balance, to architect your Business to support your life:

1. Wake Up!   –   Pick Up Your Own Yardstick. Are You Where You Want To Be?
2. Give Focus   –   Create the Living Picture of Your Desired Future State
3. Create Clarity –   Clear Vision + Clear Plan = Clear Results
4. Take Action   –   Execute. Assess. Learn. Repeat.
5. Be Accountable –   Define Steps, Define Timeline, Define Metrics

All of these steps are critical, and are best taken in the context of one over-arching element that frames them all: the ability to establish your own personal vision.

Visioning

Vision is important. *Visioning* is critical.

Most entrepreneurs understand the value of a Vision Statement as a way to capture the desired future state for your company. It's part dream, part desire, part direction. It is designed to be the inspiration, the foundation for your company's strategic planning. It is a powerful, confident pronouncement of the truth that you seek to create. Written in the present-tense, the consensus definition for Vision Statement ties it to a business.

While valuable, a Vision Statement is insufficient to inspire, to drive, to lead your company. You need to take it a step further. Your business needs a *Vision Story*.

A Vision *Story* is everything behind the Vision Statement. It captures a day-in-the-life description of your company; the operational environment, the cultural environment, leadership ethos, team demographics and dynamics. It is rich in imagery, paints a complete picture, and inspires.

But where do **you**, the entrepreneur, show up in that corporate Vision Story? What about your personal desires and plans? For most entrepreneurs, they remain invisible.

True success will elude you until you create your own, complete

Vision Story. I have experienced this personally, and in my coaching with entrepreneurs and high-performing executives.

A *complete* Vision Story is structured much like the one for your company. The difference is that this version covers the personal and the professional: family, friends, work, play, travel, food, culture, etc. It's based on what you want for your life, for your spouse, for your kids, for the family. It describes your relationships, your recreation, and your passions. It captures your work environment, work style, location, market, team culture, leadership style.

It resonates with you. It inspires you. Your heart beats faster as you read it.

As you walk through the steps to create Life-Work Balance, your Vision Story is a critical guiding resource.

You do not have to choose between having a business or having a life. You have to be intentional enough to create both. And that takes a vision that incorporates both. They do **not** have to take turns.

Architect your Business to Support your Life

1. Wake Up!

Look at your life. What's working? What's not working? What are you tolerating? What's driving you? What are you here to do? What is your purpose?

Would the child you were be proud of the adult you are?

At this stage, you will not likely have the answers to all of these questions – and when you ask them, you might not like what you see. What's important, here, is that you begin to ask yourselves questions that bring you to explore your present state. No judgment, just open exploration. Are you where you want to be?

A special note here: it is unfair to judge past behaviour, both personal and professional, based on current understanding. Compassion for yourself is critical to your success. Try this: "I forgive myself everything, knowing that I did the best that I could with what I knew at the time." It works.

2. Give Focus

"How different our lives are when we really know what is deeply important to us, and keeping that picture in mind, we manage ourselves each day to be and to do what really matters most."
~ Stephen Covey

Creating a vision story for your company brings success, both operational **and** cultural. Just as the culture of the work environment determines the success of a company, so does the culture of your life bring success as a human being. With a complete vision story for your own life, one that includes your personal and professional worlds, then you can architect your professional life to support your life.

There are no rules for formatting your Vision Stories. Some of the people create a vision board. Some create a vision narrative.

Some create a bulleted list. Some create mind-movies (a video collage). Some even distill it down to a post-it!

Regardless of the format, the real impact of the Vision Story comes from keeping it in front of you, top-of-mind, present, alive. Put up the vision board in your office, or scan it and make it your screensaver. Read the narrative in the morning. Record it and play it in the car. Put the list (or the post-it) on your bathroom mirror. Whatever works best for you, the bottom line is: keep your Vision Story alive by keeping it in front of you.

The simplest and most powerful way to use your Vision Story to shape your life and your business is a simple question. I call this *"The Threshold Filter"*:

Does this action/decision move me closer to realizing my Vision Story, or farther away from it?

Wield it like a weapon to fiercely defend the future you are creating. Cut away that which does not serve. Use it like a compass to stay relentlessly on your path. Constantly reorient yourself toward you future.

3. Create Clarity

> *"I have found that plans are useless,*
> *but planning is indispensable."*
> ~ Dwight D. Eisenhower

You no longer buy into the myth that you have to make your family work around your business. You've woken up, you've asked yourself the difficult questions, and you've painted a picture of what's important to you, and why. Now it's time to create a plan.

Planning from your vision story is critical, the ultimate expression of Stephen Covey, "start with the end in mind." You've already got a business plan. You've already got a methodology for strategic planning. You are already doing tactical planning with your team. What's different?

Start filtering **all** of those structures and processes through *"The Threshold Filter"*:

Does this action/decision move me closer to realizing my Vision Story, or farther away from it?

You've got the hard part done. You've created your vision story and you know where you're going. Using your vision story to shape your planning doesn't have to be hard. It just has to be conscious. This is some of the most rewarding work you'll ever do within your business. And it's a great place to use a coach.

A good example of a vision story is the following by one of my clients:

> After a decade in the dot com world at the executive level, my client had burned out. He left his last company to figure out what to do next. After becoming stir-crazy, he took a job working in sales on the retail floor … for $11 an hour.

We worked on creating his vision story - both personal and professional. He focused on what he wanted for himself, for his wife, for his children, for his business, for his community, even for the world. He created a vision of what life looked like at a specific point in time – 10 years out. The outcome was a rich, resonant, inspiring and clear picture of the future he committed to creating.

Now? He is in Colorado building his photography and video production company. He's doing what he loves to do, supporting his family and moving closer and closer to the reality of his Vision Story. He is also able to support his long-tem passion – he is producing his first feature-length film.

His marriage and family are thriving. He is living life fully.

Profitable Business. Thriving Family. Fulfilling life. *THAT is success.*

4. Take Action

*"We have a strategic plan here. It's called
DOING THINGS."
~ Herb Kelleher*

*"Imperfect Action is better than perfect in-action."
~ Harry Truman*

Faffing about, trying to make sure that a plan is perfect, is the most common way I experience entrepreneurs standing in their own way. I see it time and time again. It's what keeps them working hard, rather than working smart. It's what keeps them off-balance. It's what keeps them stuck.

Risk-aversion can squelch creativity, and fear of failure is paralyzing. Until you embrace failure as a tool for learning, and the gateway to creative solutions, you are driving your company to stagnation.

There is a classic story about Thomas Edison. In attempting to invent the incandescent bulb, he failed more than 1,000 times. (I've seen that number quoted as high as 5,000 or 10,000.) When asked if he was discouraged by the seemingly endless failures, Edison is rumoured to have said, "I have not failed 1,000 times. I have successfully discovered 1,000 ways to **not** make a light bulb."

Edison believed that the people who fail are the "people who did not realize how close they were to success when they gave up." Trying something risky could be the very thing that could be a game-changer for your company. Playing it safe won't get you there.

There is no success without constant imperfect action. A flawed plan, with flawless execution, will consistently outperform a flawless plan with flawed execution.
Reconnect with your Vision Story. Reconnect with your "Why." Evaluate your decisions based on The Personal Litmus Test/Criterion. And take action!

5. Be Accountable

"What gets measured, gets managed."
~ Peter Drucker

Accountability is a chapter, a book, a library unto itself. It is the topic of conferences, endless trainings, TED Talks, mind-numbing PowerPoint presentations, and more.

For now, let's keep it simple. Our Accountability Model has 5 Core Components:

1. *Mindfulness* – Be intentional. Create your own culture of accountability.
2. *Tracking* – Knowing what to track and establishing a cadence of assessment.
3. *Systems* – Internal & external; hard & soft systems; partners & patterns.
4. *Celebration* – Mark your successes AND failures: Be judgment-free. Assess & adjust.
5. *Recovery* – Use Vision Story and Values to bring yourself, your company back on track.

We use this model as a core tool when helping entrepreneurs, teams and organizations shift culture. Want to know a dirty little secret? The same accountability concepts work at home, and can dramatically impact the tone of the home.

Looking Forward

For the first part of my professional life, I lived everyone else's expectation, except my own. I didn't have a vision story of my life and what I wanted. I had pieces. It just wasn't a complete picture. I did have pieces of my own story (like my vision of a fulfilling marriage and thriving children). But I was lacking a vision of what my professional life looked like. And that carried into the way I built, managed and worked in my business.

What was missing for me was any sense of why. What's missing for you?

Now? I have a marriage that has entered a third decade, I have a business partner that I love and respect (she also happens to be my wife), we have three phenomenal children, and two growing businesses. We are moving, faster and faster, toward making our Vision Story a reality. We are living life fully. **THAT is success.**

From this moment forward, I challenge you to put your life *first,* and to commit to making your business work to support your life's Vision Story.

About David Taylor-Klaus

David Taylor-Klaus is a Husband, Father & Friend. He is a Coach, Mentor, & Speaker. He is a Serial Entrepreneur, Strategist & Visionary. He is a Wine Collector (and drinker), Avid Cyclist & Lifelong Learner.

David reintroduces Successful Entrepreneurs to their families. Through coaching, his clients overcome the overwhelming of a growing business and raising a family. His clients create the kind of Life-Work Balance the produces a *profitable business* and a *thriving family*.

David believes that a powerful leader exists in each of us. He enables his clients – both individuals and teams – to unearth & unleash that leadership and take an active, intentional, and dynamic role in their personal and professional lives.

Both his personal and professional worlds clearly reflect a journey in pursuit of excellence, always with a great deal of humor and heart. He is known for his sharp intellect and incisive ability to see what others do not. He balances fierce candor with a warm heart ... a style described as an iron fist in a velvet glove.

Touchstone Coaching was founded in 2008 by Elaine Taylor-Klaus. After selling his company to his partner, David joined Touchstone Coaching in 2009. Prior to that, David was CEO of Digital Positions, an internet strategy and web development firm he co-founded in 1995. As a strategist, he worked closely with C-level executives, senior management teams and boards of directors, coaching them through broader perspectives around how interactive initiatives support the corporate vision and values for positive growth. Prior to DP, David spent 5 years in technology consulting after a decade in hospitality.

David and Elaine currently live in Atlanta with their 3 children and a dog (named Kat) in a Buckhead neighborhood they developed in 1994.

David@TouchstoneCoaching.com

TouchstoneCoaching.com

Twitter: @ExecutiveAlly

Facebook: facebook.com/TouchstoneCoaching

(404) 822-9688

Share your experience at
http://www.facebook.com/TouchstoneCoaching

Chapter 10
Baby Steps into Your Online Brand
By Tracie Kriete

How to best start your online brand

In this chapter I will share with you some of the main areas that are important to consider when creating an online brand. I recommend a "Baby Step Method" when it comes to starting your online brand. You may start out with a website and a Facebook page, but you will evolve into having a presence on all relevant platforms.

Everyone has their own opinion on which online platform to focus on; but in my 15 years experience with SMB's, it is best to take baby steps when it comes to entering the online arena. Baby steps are necessary for many reasons; available budget, dedicated staff, level of expertise, and many more. A great aspect in today's marketing industry, it is easy to start your online brand since most of the platforms allow you to create your brand at no cost; just your time and effort.

Where do I start?

I hear this question from many of my clients. When deciding where to begin your online marketing adventure you must consider where your target audience is engaged. Are they on Facebook, Twitter, Google+, Pinterest, Instagram, and or LinkedIn? To narrow down your platforms, I have created a graph that demonstrates in general terms what audiences are using the different types of platforms:

Target Audience:	Men	Women	B2B	B2C
Platforms:				
Facebook		X		X
Twitter	X	X	X	X
Google +	X		X	X
Pinterest		X		X
Instagram	X			X
LinkedIn	X	X	X	

In the above graph you will see how the "typical" user utilizes the top Social Media platforms. There will always be that user who does not fit into the mold above, but this gives the novice online marketer a solid starting point. How your potential customers use these platforms will evolve over time, so it is important that you utilize your budget and time correctly.

How the Platforms are being used Today

Most people are familiar with the top Social Media Platforms; Facebook, Twitter, Google +, Pinterest, Instagram, and LinkedIn. A key to remember is that each user will not fit into the "perfect" user characteristics; you can only plan for the majority user. It is also important to realize that you may not use the platform that you are promoting, but your target audience is. I will give you some examples of SMB's I have created strategies for, and why I chose the platforms for the campaigns.

Company A: Regional Painting Corporation

Target Audience: CEO of Household (Women)

Phase One "Baby Step 1": Website with mobile version and Facebook Page

Reason: Women love to see testimonials and pictures. They need to know that they can "trust" their service provider. With creating the Facebook presence, the company was able to show multiple photo albums with the different services that they offer. They also were able to demonstrate their "trust-worthy" and "reliable" aspects of the company. Women want to know who is coming to their door and what to expect.

Company B "Baby Step 1": Local Bar and Pub

Target Audience: 21-45 year olds in 5 mile radius from location

Phase One: Website with mobile version, Facebook page, and Twitter page

Reason: The target customer is not going to drive more than a 5 mile distance to grab a drink. With the concentration of men and women that are using Facebook and Twitter in their target demographic, the daily posts about specials and events is easily spread, and helps to promote the location

These are just two examples of how to start. Your online brand is an evolution. You do not want to spread yourself too thin, then you cannot listen to what your customers are saying, putting you out of the conversation.

Every new company will have to determine who they are trying to reach with their message. When you have decided who you want to reach, then you can start on your check list for creating your online presence.

Starting Your Online Brand Check List

The best way that I have been able to assist my clients is by creating a "check list" of sorts. This list will help you plan your strategy, execution, and optimization of your marketing messages.

Strategy: This helps to create the content that you will be creating your online brand with, and how to best grow your online brand.

Baby Step 1:
1. What is your service area (physical area)?
2. What is your service/product offering?
3. Who is your competition?
4. How saturated is your market place?
5. What makes you different from the competition?
6. What is your competition doing currently?
7. Who in your personal network can help you share the news about your new business?
8. How much time are you able to dedicate to managing your online brand?
9. What is your comfort level with online platforms?

Baby Step 2:
1. Design your website- doesn't have to be fancy, but make sure you put "tags" in so you can show up on Google searches (indexed)
2. Create basic:
   a. About us
   b. Mission
   c. Values

  d. Key value statements

  e. Photo albums: you may or may not have all of these, but these are some good albums to start creating. Always have a camera with you, so you can document:

    i. Team

    ii. Leadership

    iii. Previous work

    iv. Before/After (if applicable)

    v. Community Involvement

  f. Specials or a list of special offers for a quarter at a time

  g. List of groups or associations you are involved in

3. Create a calendar for your Social Media Posts

  a. Plan out a month in advance, if able to

  b. Create documents that have all communications- so you can re-purpose, if needed

4. Set up Marketing email address- so you can use this in setting up all Social Media profiles

  a. This creates a stream-lined process in checking replies and communications via chosen Social Media profiles

Baby Step 3:

1. Set up Social Media Profiles (which ever are applicable)

  a. Facebook

  b. Twitter

  c. LinkedIn

  d. Pinterest

  e. Instagram

  f. Foursquare (if you are an actual location)

2. Use content from previous steps to fill out profiles

3. Set a reoccurring date on your calendar to look at analytics from profiles

Baby Step 4:

1. Monitor your networks on a daily (weekly, at minimum) basis
   a. Allows you to respond to:
      i. Requests
      ii. Comments
      iii. Complaints
      iv. Engagements
2. After the first month:
   a. Look at what is getting the most activity and optimize
   b. Use your time where your customers are interacting with you the most.
3. Expand your brand into additional platforms

If you follow the Baby Steps, you can safely enter the world of online branding. You must remember that Social Media takes time to show results. Slow and steady wins the race. If you have any additional questions or need advice, feel free to email me at **tracie.kriete@yahoo.com**

About Tracie-Ruth Kriete, MSM

Tracie began her career as a web designer/graphic artist in the mid-90s after graduating from Indiana University and Purdue University. She has been involved in all aspects of marketing throughout her career including public relations, promotions, graphic design, sales, and product development. After receiving her Masters in Management, Tracie evolved her career into more of a market leadership/development role. After leaving Louisville, KY where she developed marketing/advertising campaigns for SMB's, she moved to Atlanta, GA in 2005 to help in the launch of Cox Enterprises' new online search directory, Kudzu.com. While with Cox, Tracie was involved in market strategy, sales leadership, sales training and management of expansion markets. Not only did Tracie build the foundation for the sales department, she worked with her local clients to develop and execute online marketing campaigns for SMB.

In 2009 Tracie started her own freelance consulting firm, 'Brand Bouquet', which specializes in Social Media strategy, execution, and optimization. Tracie is currently the Vice President of Marketing for the Atlanta Interactive Marketing Association (AIMA) and is also on the Advisory Board for the United Way's Cause Marketing Committee. During the day she heads up the Social Media side of Crawford Media Services, as well as traveling the Southeast visiting clients. She specializes in all things interactive: social, display, search, mobile, and video. In her spare time she loves to travel, read, and practice photography.

Chapter 11
How Listening is the Key to Money, Love and Happiness

By Rene Kamstra

One of the most frequent things I always get asked about is, "What is your most valuable tool in running multiple successful businesses?" I then tell the person who asked me that it's quite simple and there is no fancy software or education to be had – the key to running a successful business, or any other part of your life, is listening. With 5 thriving businesses in my belt and clients in almost 30 countries, I believe I can back up my claim.

The central feature to any transaction is to talk only 10 to 20 percent of the time and leave out the rest for the other party's discourse. Not only will you be able to build rapport much faster, but it also clues you in on what type of services they require. This then will enable you to earn their trust at a more accelerated pace than normal and will open new doors of opportunity for you.

Unbeknownst to many, listening is actually one of the most powerful tools anyone can use in their quest to achieving success since building relationships – both in your business and personal life – is a pivotal advantage when it comes to establishing effective communication, impressive sales process and being happy.

I believe that once this tried and tested skill is mastered, individuals in organizations of every size will be able to improve their depth of trust with both their existing clients and potential customers. Moreover, they will also be able to move themselves to make a vast headway into reaching out to their clients, which will then invariably lead to rapid increase in revenue for the long-term. On another note, listening also works magic with people in one's personal lives as it paves the way for better and well-meaning relationships.

How Businesses Employ the Power of Listening

To illustrate my aforementioned points, a critical foundation of mom and pop businesses are rooted in proper greeting by acknowledging a customer's presence the moment they set foot in the establishment, no matter how busy they are. This alone shows a basic understanding that you value their patronage and you are grateful for their presence. This kind of genuine connection is where opportunities lie in today's business environment since all other companies are concerned with making the biggest profit with nary a concern for their clients.

The companies that are best positioned for massive growth in the years to come are the ones who dare to connect to their target market by investing in getting to know what their audience wants. Contrary to the common conception, there is power in utilizing the feminine energy in one's sales process instead of solely going by with an aggressive, masculine approach. By placing value on nurturing rapport along with building trust and loyalty with your customers, it will then inevitably lead to word of mouth marketing that's powerful and cost-effective in driving revenue, more so than any high-profile campaign.

New Era of Marketing

Consumers of today are more wary of how they are being marketed to, particularly because of the availability of information through social media – they know whether a business is true to their claims and if they sincerely value their customers. Companies that are investing in listening to their customers are able to develop greater trust in building their relationships. Some such examples of this are Zappos, Apple and Starbucks, to name a few. These are all companies that are excellent at listening and taking action in making their patrons happy.

The Consequences of Failing to Listen

There are a number of challenges that can emerge whenever we are not in active listening mode. Here are a few examples:

- You lose your ability to effectively influence, persuade and negotiate.
- Conflicts and arguments can arise.
- It can lead to misunderstanding.
- Being unable to see the other's perspective.
- The responses between you and the other party can be disconnected.
- You focus more on reacting instead of reciprocating an answer to what the other person said.
- The other party can feel used once they think that what they have to say is no matter of consequence to you.
- There will be a lot of interruptions because the two of you are not meeting eye to eye.

By becoming a better listener however, you will be able to strengthen your ability to affect, convince and broker more favorable terms for you and the other party. Personally, I believe that listening is the key to having "Big Sales and Loyal Customers that stay with me and refer me for years." All of these are no doubt necessary for workplace success!

Today's Culture Imbalance

We are bombarded every day, both personally and professionally, with information overload. A lot of our interpersonal relationships are only being cultivated through technological means like texting, emailing, instant messaging and even social media sites.

While it's always good to be able to have free access to information, our increased reliance on these mediums for our business relationships creates an imbalance between two elements of communication – that of speaking and listening. For my part, I see this as a disparity between masculine and feminine energy because when we look at the development of our species as a whole, it can be said that technological development mirrors masculine energy while spiritual development can be tagged as the feminine side.

Just as balance is necessary for one's physiological health, it is also equally important for us as a whole, to maintain equilibrium in both our technological and spiritual development. As a result of this disparity, the scale has tipped perilously to developing just the technological side. In the same way that the influx of information increases, the more we feel alienated and ignored like no one is listening or paying attention to us.

We can see this blatantly with businesses that have done away with good customer service. The more time we spend with technology, the less time we spend developing deeper personal relationships outside of it, which can then be detrimental to one's spiritual psyche. This is why developing both is vital to connecting with the people in our lives – both professionally and personally.

Building Deeper Rapport with Others

It all starts with mastering good open-ended questions that encourage the other party to disclose more about their selves. After which, all you have to do is to listen attentively. There is an art and science behind good listening and it is a seldom occurrence to come across a person who possesses this trait, either in business or social occasions, that it takes most people by surprise.

Listening has to come from a place of no judgment since it is understandable that people would inevitably speak from their own perspective, and it's the best they know how. Conflict, misunderstanding, and criticism all come from a standpoint of thinking that you know better than the other party.

We should never put our own meaning into what other people are saying because it'll only espouse adverse reactions instead of pro-active communication. If we can stop our reactions and take the time out to ask questions that will clarify, then that's the only time we can reach a deeper level of understanding.

Communication at this level is not only invaluable, but also immeasurable, as well. It is unconditional and leaves room for growth, trust and ingenuity, or even billion dollar profits. Imagine if IBM had only listened to Bill Gates when he started with Windows.

The Continuum of Communication

a) Ask a question
b) Listen to the answer
c) Ask a follow-up question that delves deeper
d) Adapt to the direction of conversation

Tip 1: If you can attain the mastery of listening at this level then people are bound to believe that you heard them and that you sincerely want to be able to help them. By asking and listening to the other party, you will be able to find out what it is they need. In essence, an effective sales pitch is not about employing sweet-talk or high-pressure sales tactics but simply, it is all about having good listening skills.

Tip 2: Good communication skills require a high level of self-awareness since it is in understanding one's personal style of connection that will enable us to leave lasting impressions with the people we come into contact in our lives. For a free disc-flex report, just email Rene at **renekamstra3@gmail.com**.

Tip 3: If you're communicating over the phone and you can hear background noise, as if they are engaged in another activity, use a tie down question to pull them back in. A good thing to say would be, "It sounds like you've got little ones, how old are they?" or "I hear Skype in your background. Do you mind if we can just focus for a few minutes on this conversation." After which, share them a statistic stating that only 20% of what we do brings 80% of results, and go on to tell them how you would love that conversation to fall into the best results ever category.

Five Key Elements to Active Listening

The five key elements to active listening fundamentally help you to ensure that the other person knows you are hearing what they say. Here are the following tips you can keep to for better listening:

1. Pay attention.
   Give the speaker your undivided attention and acknowledge what they're trying to say. This doesn't have to be strictly about verbal communication because in actuality, words only comprise 7% of communication.
2. Show that you are listening.
   Direct your body language and gestures to convey your attention.
3. Provide feedback.
   Oftentimes, our own personal filters, assumptions and belief can distort what we hear. As a listener, your role is to understand what is being said by reflecting on what is being said by asking questions and following these steps:
   - Paraphrase by saying, "What I'm hearing is..." and "Sounds like you are saying..."
   - Clarify certain points by saying, "Is that what you mean?" and "Tell me more."

- It would also do good to summarize the speaker's comments from time to time.
4. Defer judgment.
   Interrupting is a waste of time because it frustrates the speaker and it limits full understanding of the message the other is trying to convey.
5. Respond appropriately.
   Active listening is a model of respect and understanding and it also helps you gain information and see their perspective. There is nothing to be gained by attacking the person, so asserting one's opinions diplomatically is the best way to go.

Being a Better Communicator

It takes a good amount of concentration and determination to be an active listener. One needs to set aside all other thoughts and ensure that they understand the message since without this important skill, one might find that what someone said and what they heard are two very different things.

Start using active listening today to become a better communicator, which in turn can help you improve your workplace productivity and to develop better relationships.

If by any chance you find yourself responding emotionally to what someone said, it would be advisable to first ask for more information by saying, "I may not be understanding you correctly and I find myself taking what you said personally" and then elucidate the points you think you heard and follow it up with a question asking, "Is this what you mean?"

On average, research shows that we can hear four times faster than we can talk and therefore, we have the ability to sort ideas at an accelerated pace in our mind. This is why as your listening skills improve, so will your aptitude for conversation, too. To exemplify this, a friend of mine named Pamela Hermann once got a compliment stating how great her communication skills are. Although she hadn't said more than four words, she had listened to the other person for the whole duration of their conversation.

Basically, one of the best solutions to business success is easy, cost-free and only entails a change of perception.

About Rene Kamstra

Rene Kamstra brings a unique worldview to her many roles as media personality, author, speaker, radio show host and business executive. Born in South Africa, by Dutch parents, Ms. Kamstra is a dual Psychology and Education graduate of the University of South Africa, holds top certification from the Royal College of Music in London and now lives in New York City. She currently coaches and teaches businesses on 6 continents as an Executive Master Coach for Tony Robbins and Chet Holmes Company – "Business Breakthroughs International". She is also the Director of Consulting for 7 Figure Speaking Empire, where she does sales and sales training for big ticket items on a daily basis. In fact, sales and connecting with people is her passion. Using methods from Chet Holmes, Tony Robbins, Jay Abraham and many other teachers, she has grown the sales training division of her company to a point where no one can compete.

The energy and the fun she brings to the table, as well as her insight into people is what made her a very successful and sought after coach. Ms. Kamstra's private practice currently serves clients throughout the world. Her "Rene Radio" show and new book "Going It Alone" feature amazing accomplishments by everyday individuals, like the ones she encounters in her philanthropic work with Down Syndrome awareness, the Shriver

Family, and Special Olympics, as well as serving as CFO for the "Wellness Connection", a non-profit group to help abused spouses and children.

renekamstra3@gmail.com.

Chapter 12
Bring Your "A" Game
By Sandra Saenz

Moderate verses Extraordinary

Your life is a result of all your choices. Yep, Newsflash! I did say "your" choices. You are continuously choosing how you spend your time and what you will do with those golden moments. ..So make them count! Make them extraordinary. By the time you finish reading this exact sentence, this exact moment in time is gone, spent, and used forever. Think about it. Good news. You're on the right track to extraordinary. You picked up this book. We are making choices every single moment of every day. One choice, one decision can change your life . . .for the rest of your life.

Of course, I realize there are small choices and big choices right?

Really ???

Beeeeep, wrong! All of our choices impact our lives on some level. There are no small choices. The truth is, we are deciding, selecting, sorting through our choices every moment. We are where we are today – as a result of all our choices. Our life, our career is where it is now – because we have chosen it. We really are the Director of our own movie. So why not create it exactly the way we want it to be?

Employers now are not settling for computer technicians, or specialists; they are actually posting job ads for "Computer Ninjas" ... i.e., extraordinary performers. The use of the word

"Ninja" related to employee ads has exploded by 7000%, according to the Huffington Post. O.K., granted, not all of us have a burning desire to be considered a "Ninja", but you get the point. Having the passion and drive to go the extra mile and be extraordinary at this time where information and resources are at our fingertips – is not only noticeable, is not only enjoyable, it's a must.

Remember, doing things in "moderation" leads to a Moderate life, a Moderate business contribution.

So when I hear people making excuses about actions which may take them off track from their "A" Game, I wonder if they realize it? I hear phrases something like "Well yes, I normally don't do this. I know it's not good for me ... only in moderation." "I don't typically eat this, or don't think like this ...only in moderation."
I am thinking to myself – Really???

Making choices with awareness is paramount to Bringing Your "A" Game into play. Do you desire a moderate life? Or do you desire a phenomenal life? Do you wish for an extraordinary career, or a moderate career? Do you want to have happiness and success in your life & business.... in moderation?"

All of our choices are significant. So, for someone to choose YOU as a business partner – you must
- believe you're significant
- behave like you are significant
- perform as you are significant.....

.......therefore,

Bring your "A" Game! ... or stay home.

*"Nothing splendid has ever been achieved except
by those who dared believe that something
inside of them was superior to circumstance."*
~ Bruce Barton ~

Everybody has an "A" Game. Here are 6 key steps in bringing your "A" Game, with a secret weapon ingredient included. In Stephen Covey's book, The 8th Habit, a survey of 2.5 million people related to managers & effectiveness, research showed that only 14% "stay diligently focused on their most important goals". Incredible. This is a very low number considering all the talk of priorities in leadership. From my experience in conducting leadership trainings all over the globe, I must confess I think this number is pretty accurate.

Most people (not just leaders) are in a reactive mode verses a proactive mode. We are being constantly bombarded with information and crisis situations to solve. The following 6 step Game Plan immediately puts you in proactive mode.

The Game Plan to Extraordinary

Get Crystal Clear
Get clear on what you desire. Clarity is Power! Real power. Clarity for yourself, who you are, and what you can contribute. From my 20+ years experience in advertising, I learned the strength of a power brand is the undeniable clarity of that brand's USP (unique selling point). Once that clear USP is established and consistently communicated and delivered, it's super easy to bring the "A" Game. Ask yourself "what is my USP?" When Federal Express first started out in the early 70's they focused on "overnight delivery". This became their USP,

and nobody could touch them. Since then, they've expanded their services, but they will always be thought of as "the" overnight originators. It's easy to bring your "A" game when you are clear WHO you are and WHAT you bring to the table. I love the example my colleague in retail asks his 300+ employees, "How do we know you were here today?"

Start with the MVP

Now that you're clear on your focus and what you contribute (which is extraordinary of course!)... check in with your MVP (most valuable player) – that's YOU. To set up a winning game plan, do the internal work first. In other words, before taking all kinds of action, make sure you are on the right channel on the inside. This step is the secret weapon ingredient, mentioned earlier.

This is a bit different from a focused vision. Don't just see it, as in a vision (which is very powerful, by the way)...but go the extra step and "be it" already. Start with your attitude, your passion, and your core. Do whatever it takes to live and feel that successful "A" Game as if it already exists. Talk to yourself about how wonderful the end result is and feel your way there. Let's say you have a specific Fortune 500 company you'd like to do business with. Pretend it has already happened. Play with the ideas of ...how does that impact me? How do I impact them? How would I behave? What would be different? Dive into the channel of your "A" Game. Your attitude, mood and drive affect every part of your life. And it is paramount to your fulfillment of anything. In Dale Carnegie's philosophy of development, to produce skills/habits/results – the first step is "attitude". Think of it, you can teach someone a skill like typing, but attitude comes from within. So start from within for long term "A" Game behaviour ... start with your MVP – YOU!

"Success is not to be pursued;
it is to be attracted by the person you become."
~Leo Tolstoy~

Have a Game Plan

So much has been written about the benefits of having a concrete strategy and plan. Since we're extraordinary, let's focus on what makes an "A Game" plan. We could be working very hard, even working efficiently and still be moving in the wrong direction without a plan. It's like the difference in an action list and a result oriented list. I've known many people who can accomplish a long list of actions with no results towards their goal! Keep your eye on the ball. A good game plan consists of the following:

- All action steps contribute in some way to the targeted goal. If you've done step one and are clear, then this is simple. Otherwise we can become sidetracked into short term gratification.
- You've considered all your resources. Ensure you are using all the people, ideas, and techniques which are within your reach. Most people try to do too much themselves... Ego.
- Anticipate and plan for the challenges. Be ready for the curve balls and have a strategy for how you'll handle them. Minimize the surprises. This keeps you in proactive mode.
- Keep the MVP happy and motivated. Do whatever it takes to fuel your drive and energy. This is different for everyone. Find out what your hot buttons are.

"The whole world steps aside for the man
who knows where he is going."
~Anonymous~

Take Action

This is a step where many start to slow down. We have fabulous attitude, a desired target, but we hesitate, procrastinate, and everything else before just getting down to the business of doing. It's like everyone who wants to get in shape or quit smoking – people want to do it, they know what they need to do, but just getting there. Do whatever it takes to get your momentum going. Remember, "knowing" and "doing" are 2 very different things. Most people find that once they start, it's much easier than they thought. Here's a hint. The action step will just flow into being when you are pumped by the passion of being on the right channel on the inside (which was previously #2 of your "A" Game). When you can feel the applause, the standing ovation, and hear the accolades, you won't have any trouble hitting it out of the park.

As John W Raper said *"....then you can take your time going around the bases."*

Here, I'd like to recommend Brian Tracey's book <u>Eat that Frog</u>.

Check the Score

This is a quality control for yourself. A reality check on how your "A" Game is progressing will keep you on track. In this step, it is very important to be brutally honest with yourself, and get feedback from appropriate and objective sources. Insert this as an integral milestone to your game plan. Ask yourself "What's working, what's not working, what's missing". If the pulse you take is fabulous, you will be even more inspired. If the pulse is weak, then you will be aware you need to change the play. Either way – it's a score you need to know. An important note here: even though I am using the word "score" – your method of measurement isn't always going to be the "numbers". It will also be how you "feel" about what you've contributed in your game, and how others feel about your contribution. This is the real key to spiral you into extraordinary territory… your fulfillment. I just saw a clever TV advertisement about a pair of jeans. Think of your score like a good pair of jeans – don't focus on the number, focus on how the jeans make you feel when you're in them. Your measurement of success is how you feel and how others feel.

Celebrate Your Victories!

You'll notice I put "victories", plural. Yes, you will have many when you bring your "A" Game. Recognizing wins and rewarding ourselves is the important for several reasons.

- It allows us to stop and lock in the feeling and energy of victory, so we can repeat it over and over.
- It is a turbo charged driver for momentum, which flows over into other actions, projects and even people. After a success, it seems everything you touch shines brighter.
- It's an opportunity to recognize your team and all those involved in bringing your "A" Game to life. You really don't do much by yourself, you know. (wink)

So, while you're getting your MVP player pumped up and in the zone, start daydreaming about how you'll celebrate. How will you reward yourself? New York Giants' wide receiver, Victor Cruz has his signature "salsa dance" with each touchdown. What will your Victory Dance look like?

Your personal "A" Game can only be played and offered by you. There is no one else on the planet exactly like you…

The Hero Within, Dr. Carol S. Pearson

"Perhaps you do not see yourself as being talented, smart, advantaged enough to matter to the world. If so, you run the risk of giving away your power and letting others carry the day. ....If you do so, it is not only you who loses; the society loses, because the gift that only you can bring.... will be lost."

It's O.K. to listen to mentors, colleagues, coaches, and even competitors, but it's absolutely CRITICAL to listen to your heart, your passion, your inner guidance, and yep, your gut! Your instincts will always be right on the mark. They never let you down when you follow your truth. And this strength you encounter when you follow your truth is never, ever, ever, in "moderation". It will always delight and surprise you with how everyone and everything conspires to bring your "A" Game into play! And guess what... usually... what you desire is NEVER in moderation. The heart and soul know no boundaries. Somewhere inside -- you know that there is an unlimited abundance of everything to accomplish whatever you wish.

**"Moderation"?? , nope, I will skip it, thank you very much ----
I don't even want it "on the side"!** ✧

The important thing to remember is that you are continuously influencing your direction. No matter how much you blame others, you give away your power to others, you make excuses . ...You are in control. You are responsible. You have the power to shape your destiny right now, and at each moment --- including the few minutes it took you to read these pages. So now you know . . . .

And there is no going back.

* * *

Keys to Bringing Your "A" Game!

1. Be yourself, that's the best you can ever be. (Be like someone else, you'll always be 2nd)
2. Go the extra mile: when you think you've done everything, do something more!
3. Own your relationships: Take responsibility for what's working and what's not working. Remember, you're half of the equation.
4. Do it BIG or don't do it at all!
5. Ask and then be quiet and Listen! Practice the 70/30 rule. Listen 70% & talk 30%.
6. Do something for someone else without expecting anything in return.
7. Use the element of surprise... this keeps them engaged & curious for more.
8. Trust your voice. Speaking from your heart with authentic generosity is a shortcut to understanding.
9. Use the Power of "we". When we take action with an inclusive benefit for all, it's powerful. It should always be a "win/win" environment.
10. Watch your focus – Put yourself in their map of the world.
11. Put your ego in the back seat, and don't let it be a back seat driver!
12. Always, always take the high road – maintain integrity. Remember you are *extraordinary*!
13. Be clear who you are and what you stand for, and others will be clear and respect you.
14. Be grateful and say it! Remember, they can do business with anyone they choose.
15. Think long-term. Everything in life is long-term.

About Sandra Saenz

Sandra Saenz has been called a "Provocational" Business Coach & Speaker, provoking people to come into their own realizations and take action towards their personal empowerment. Her interactive and energetic training style has taken her from Rio de Janeiro to Copenhagen, Singapore, Moscow and Vienna -- among some of her groups all over the globe.

Ms. Saenz, originally from Texas, is a former business executive with 20+ years experience in marketing/advertising. In a moment of inspired clarity (her theme), while conducting business development meetings in Europe, she accepted a project offer and moved from Nashville to Budapest, Hungary in 1994. Since then she has been living in Europe part of the year and expanding her Training/Coaching practice with a variety of well known multi-national clients. She is the owner of **Dream Team Communications,** as well as a **Global Dale Carnegie Trainer.** She has currently been named **Top Business Trainer** for the 4th consecutive year in her sponsor franchise country of Austria, and for the 2nd year ranked in **the Top 1% in EMEA** (Europe, Middle East and Asia.)

Sandra's philosophy revolves around her theme, **"Clarity is Power"**! She combines her extensive strategic branding experience from the international advertising world, where she supervised 8 countries while working at Ogilvy & Mather in Vienna, with the dynamic techniques of her theater & communications background. The result is an atmosphere filled with AHA moments, laughter, interaction, and concrete results.

Clients: She has worked with a wide variety of industries. Some of her many clients include General Motors, BMW, IBM, Kraft Foods, Procter & Gamble, Unilever, Ford, American Express, Philips, AT&T, City of New York, Embassy of South Africa, Erste Bank in Austria, Erber Group Worldwide, and Maersk Shipping & Oil Global.

Some of her TOPICS:

Leadership	Generosity Based Negotiation/Sales
Self Development	Breaking the Code: Your Personality
Presentation Skills	Your Dream Life –Taking Action
Self Confidence/Awareness	Decision Making - Values
Creating Your Personal Brand	Your Vision…NOT everyone else's!

One Continent is not enough!

Sandra has been living in Hungary and Austria since 1994, and spends half of the year in the United States in her Arizona home. Sandra speaks English, Spanish, and Hungarian.

Techniques from a variety of philosophies – from Austria, Spain, Germany, India, Hungary, Africa, Brazil, & the USA.

She currently conducts Group Workshops as well as Personal Executive Coaching.

Sandra Saenz

Global Training/Business Coach/Provocational Speaker

Dream Team Communications

US: 480-452-7902   **EUR:** +36-209-730-466

Skype: Sandra Saenz Europe

Sandra@saenzcommunication.com

Website: **www.saenzcommunication.com**

USA - Austria - Spain - Moscow - Brazil - Singapore -Chile - Africa - More...

Chapter 13
The Most Important Business Book.....Yours
by Carolyn & Mike Lewis

For thousands of years authors have been regarded with respect and admiration. And since they wrote the book, one word always came to mind....expert.

Authors tend to find themselves in the crowd that is the "cream of the crop". Being an author is the definitive demarcation line of attack, as it truly separates you from the pack. Whether you decide to write your own book, use a ghostwriter, or be included in a Multi Author book with other leaders, there's no better way for you to create yourself as an authority. Once your potential customers realize that you are a published expert, they will be ready to work with you, as well as refer others to you..

Most authors do not write their books for the money. Believe it or not, there really is very little money in books, unless you are a J.K.Rowling or Donald Trump. In the real world of book writing, the actual purpose isn't the book. It's all about what the book **will do for you**. It's all about the new opportunities that will be created, as well as all the doors that will finally open for you.

Let's explore some of the concrete benefits that becoming a published author will afford you:
- New-found respect and admiration
- Personal satisfaction
- Enhanced credibility

- Expert status with your customers
- New customer surge due to your increased credibility
- Businesses, opportunities, and people will naturally seek you out
- High sense of accomplishment
- Newfound connections and increased earnings

Can you see the awesome benefits that being an author will afford you? Being an author can double, triple, or even quadruple your chances of getting every customer you meet as a client. You'll profit from being an author for your entire life. And no one can take that away from you.

Look around you. Have you ever noticed how authors kind of seem to "strut their stuff"? Call it confidence! They tend to carry themselves a little bit differently because they, as well as others, perceive them as different. It's not ego but the knowledge that they are viewed differently because they are the expert in their field.

Credibility and esteem are what give authors this little "strut". This is an invaluable tool, which used properly, can translate into $$$$$$. When your customers trust their source, it makes it possible for them to make important decisions in their business.

The trust and authority granted to authors is already formed in the minds of the public, as well as the media. This knowledge is worth more than a king's ransom! This knowledge should be the foremost reason for becoming an author. Like we stated earlier, it's all about the new opportunities, the previously closed doors opening, and enhanced business relationships that being an author creates. All this answers the question of "Why should I become a published author"?

Think about it. Would you rather work with an "Average Joe", or an "Author/Expert"? Of course you'd rather do business with the expert. So would the majority of the population. Writing a book will allow you to STAND OUT from your competition....and put you at the level of all the other leaders that you have admired.

About a year ago a friend of ours, Dave, was offered a website building job from one of our other friends, Brad. He wasn't sure about going for the interview, because he was already putting in long hours at his business. But this was an awesome job of rebuilding and monitoring the entire website for a major firm and all their branches.

While Brad was working with the corporate office on the website candidates, we were talking with Dave about the power of having a book, and what it would do for not only his business, but also for his credibility. After much cajoling, we finally convinced him to let us do a book for him. He never realized how much that book would eventually impact his life.

Dave was the third of three candidates interviewed, but by a little "dumb luck" he was aware of the proposals from the other two candidates. Not really wanting the job because he had so little free time, he raised his proposal several thousand dollars. Going into the interview feeling confident that he would **not** get the job, Dave went in very relaxed, introduced himself, and proceeded to hand his book out as his business card. Even though the interview went well, Dave figured that with his proposal being the highest, there was no way he would be getting the job.

Two days later he received a call letting him know that indeed, the job was his. He was speechless and a bit confused. Why did they hire the most expensive person? He knew he was good and could do the job, but did he have the time?

After weighing the pros and cons, he figured that the money was good, and the job not so difficult for him, so he accepted the offer.

About a month later, he was talking with the Senior VP and came right out and asked him why he was hired. The answer shocked him. The VP said "We are a billion dollar company. Money is really no object to us, so money was not really the issue when we decided to hire someone. You were the only one who came in to the interview with their own book. This showed us that you had knowledge about your field, took pride in your work, and that you were the expert that we needed". He went on to say that "the head of the division still had his book sitting on his credenza". How powerful is that?

It took a while for this to sink in, but once it did, Dave called us and apologized for the hard time he gave us about doing the book, and explained the conversation he had with the Senior VP. He said "you were so right. Many times I took hours wooing potential clients, only to be rejected. Here I walked in with a book, and almost immediately they made up their mind that I was the right person for the job. Incredible!"

Dave's only struggle at this point was how he was going to work on this project, while keeping his other clients happy. Well, the increase in money from the new job allowed him to bring in some extra help, which freed him up for his new client. With the extra help, he was also able to take in a few more clients.

A year later, Dave is still working with the Company, hired more associates, gained more clients, and actually works less hours.

Do you think that Dave would have gotten the job if he didn't have his book? Maybe, maybe not. But he now credits the fact that his credibility actually came from being a published author. The bottom line is that being an author automatically makes you an expert. If you want an advantage over your competitors....then become a published author and brand yourself as the business expert in your niche.

There is no greater branding, or client enticement, than being a published author.

Become a published author today.

About Carolyn Lewis

Carolyn Lewis has the experience it takes to run a dynamic organization. From her first brush with the internet, to her management skills of launching AOL discs to your mailbox, and her ever increased move up the corporate ladder, this culminated as Chief Financial Officer of their $100million Land Development Company.

Carolyn has a diverse business background in such areas as finance, marketing, management, human resources and production, including owning and operating her own businesses.

After the fall of the Real Estate Market, Carolyn and her husband Michael lost their Land Development business and various building projects all over the southeast to the tune of a $60 Million bankruptcy.

Not the type to sit back and be crushed by unavoidable circumstances, it was time to re-evaluate and re-invent. Since Real Estate was totally out of the picture, the next logical step was the internet. After a slow start, some hits, and some misses, Carolyn and her husband knew that with both their backgrounds, the perfect fit was out there.

So after a diligent review of many different business opportunities, the one that seemed to spark a fire was the potential to impact people's lives with a published book. Coupled with the enjoyment she receives from working with other professionals, as well as the obvious choice that this was a great business model convinced Carolyn that this is where she wants to be.

With a true passion and desire for helping entrepreneurs to "take it to the next level", Carolyn is here to assist you in producing your printed book, therefore accomplishing your goal to become the "best of the best" in your field.

Contact Carolyn directly at **clewis@nomadceo.com** for more information on how you, too, can join the ranks as a published author.

About Mike Lewis, "The Book Guy"

Mike has over 35 years of experience in marketing, finance, construction and real estate. He previously owned and operated several companies in the southeast, including a $100 million land development company.

He is the owner / publisher of Nomad CEO, the top Ghost Publishing firm in the world, specializing in books, tools, and resources for entrepreneurship and small businesses.

His products are practical, hands-on, and based on the real-world experiences of successful entrepreneurs, CEOs, investors, lenders, and seasoned business experts.

Mike's passion for turning non-writers into authors of printed books in less than 30 days, with virtually no writing on their part, positively impacts and changes lives.

Using his complete "Done For You" publishing service has helped raise his client-author's authority and recognition in all phases of their businesses.

Check out Mike's website at www.nomadceo.com, or contact him directly at **mlewis@nomadceo.com** for information on how you, too, can become the expert in your field through the power of becoming a published author.

Visit us at www.nomadceo.com.

Resource Page
To Help You Promote Your Passion

1) Get Your Custom Mobile App today!
   http://www.yourmobileappshop.com

2) Become a Published Author
   http://www.PYPPublishingGroup.com

3) Build Your List Through Mobile Marketing
   http://www.CaptureYourAudience.com

4) Get Your Own Branded Publishing App For Facebook
   http://www.SetYourStatus.com

5) Get Your Business Website Up For Free
   http://www.BestFreeBlogsite.com

6) Sending a Card Has Never Been So Easy
   http://www.CreateACardOnline.com

7) Customized Email Signatures
   http://www.setyoursignature.com

Conversations With Experts

SPEAKER CONTACT INFO:

NOTES:

ACTIONABLE IDEAS:

SPEAKER CONTACT INFO:

NOTES:

ACTIONABLE IDEAS:

SPEAKER CONTACT INFO:

NOTES:

ACTIONABLE IDEAS:

SPEAKER CONTACT INFO:

NOTES:

ACTIONABLE IDEAS:

SPEAKER CONTACT INFO:

NOTES:

ACTIONABLE IDEAS:

SPEAKER CONTACT INFO:

NOTES:

ACTIONABLE IDEAS:

NOTES:

NOTES:

NOTES:

NOTES:

ACTION ITEMS

ACTION ITEMS

SPECIAL CONTACTS

Name:

Email:

Phone:

Skype:

Summarize Meeting:

Name:

Email:

Phone:

Skype:

Summarize Meeting:

Name:

Email:

Phone:

Skype:

Summarize Meeting:

Name:

Email:

Phone:

Skype:

Summarize Meeting:

SPECIAL CONTACTS

Name:

Email:

Phone:

Skype:

Summarize Meeting:

Name:

Email:

Phone:

Skype:

Summarize Meeting:

Name:

Email:

Phone:

Skype:

Summarize Meeting:

Name:

Email:

Phone:

Skype:

Summarize Meeting:

SPECIAL CONTACTS

Name:

Email:

Phone:

Skype:

Summarize Meeting:

Name:

Email:

Phone:

Skype:

Summarize Meeting:

Name:

Email:

Phone:

Skype:

Summarize Meeting:

Name:

Email:

Phone:

Skype:

Summarize Meeting:

SPECIAL CONTACTS

Name:

Email:

Phone:

Skype:

Summarize Meeting:

Name:

Email:

Phone:

Skype:

Summarize Meeting:

Name:

Email:

Phone:

Skype:

Summarize Meeting:

Name:

Email:

Phone:

Skype:

Summarize Meeting:

Made in the USA
Lexington, KY
27 September 2012